Out and about

a teacher's guide
to safety
on educational visits

Evans / Methuen Educational

First published September 1972 for the Schools Council
by Evans Brothers Limited
Montague House, Russell Square, London WC1B 5BX
and Methuen Educational Limited
11 New Fetter Lane, London EC4P 4EE
Reprinted (with corrections) January 1973

Distributed in the US by Citation Press
Scholastic Magazines Inc., 50 West 44th Street
New York, NY 10036
and in Canada by Scholastic–TAB Publications Ltd
123 Newkirk Road
Richmond Hill, Ontario

SBN 423 86610 9

Printed in Great Britain by
Richard Clay (The Chaucer Press) Ltd
Bungay, Suffolk

Contents

Drawings are by Peter Edwards

Foreword

The Geography Committee of the Schools Council, concerned initially about safety precautions in fieldwork, considered the general increase in out-of-school activities in many areas of the school curriculum and the need for guidance for teachers undertaking such activities. With the co-operation of other Schools Council subject committees, a working party was set up in December 1968 to prepare a publication on the safety aspects of outside activities.

This guide is based on the working party's view that safety is inextricably linked with efficient planning, organization, and supervision. No attempt has been made to conceal the problems and even possible dangers that may arise during out-of-school visits. In pointing out the problems and dangers, however, we have tried to avoid discouraging enthusiasm with prohibitions in our attempt to offer guidance on planning for safety. We have also included a brief, general description of the teacher's legal position; it is intended, though, only for guidance and does not purport to be definitive or exhaustive.

Out and About is intended primarily for teachers in England and Wales undertaking out-of-school visits for the first time. To the many experienced teachers who organize visits on a more liberal basis than we have suggested, allowing pupils greater freedom and thus greater responsibility, some of our suggestions may appear restrictive. Through such suggestions, however, we hope to promote the initial confidence and security that derive from meticulous planning and organization. We have sought to provide an authoritative and comprehensive guide for teachers: our concern has been for the safety and well-being of all the participants in out-of-school activities, for the establishment of sympathetic relationships between home, school, and community, and for the conservation of the environment into which pupils are taken.

Although prepared primarily for teachers in school, we trust that this guide will be of use to teachers in further education, to leaders of youth organizations, and to all those who organize visits and excursions for children and young people.

The chairman, Mr Wilkie Burdon, and the members of the working party are grateful for the assistance and co-operation given by organizations

9

directly concerned with the many aspects of outdoor education, local education authorities in England and Wales, professional bodies, and in particular those immediately concerned with accident prevention. They are also most grateful to Mrs M. E. G. Black of the City of Cardiff College of Education for her help in editing this guide.

Members of the working party

Wilkie Burdon (Chairman)	Warden, City of Cardiff Outdoor Pursuits Centre, Porthcawl, Glamorgan
Mrs M. E. G. Black	City of Cardiff College of Education
P. C. Boate	Pool Hayes Comprehensive School, Willenhall, Staffordshire
W. S. Brace	Elgin High School, Gateshead
C. Corner	Former Field Officer, Schools Council
J. Disley	Surrey Local Education Authority
Mrs N. Filtness	Catford County Secondary School, London SE6
W. R. A. Ellis	Sheffield Institute of Education
Y. Williams	Braintree College of Further Education

I. The development of out-of-school activities

The educational thought that gave rise to our older school buildings was one that regarded school life and life 'outside' as separate entities and sought, in attitudes and curricula as well as in building design, to perpetuate the separation. Windows were high, often frosted, so that pupils should not be distracted by the outside view from concentrating on the 'essentials' taught within the classroom. School doors and gates with high railings were often locked during the school session and children were released only at its end. History, geography, science, English, and mathematics were subjects to be studied from printed books and blackboard summaries; they bore no relationship to the town, the countryside, and the community of the children's outside life.

Our newer school buildings reflect our change of attitude towards the function and purpose of education. Their large, low windows looking out on the world symbolize a philosophy that views education and life as inseparable. In both the new and the old buildings, teachers are now working towards a closer relationship between school, environment, and community.

The schools are outward-looking, their classes increasingly 'outward-going'. Pupils are taken outside school premises on visits of varying distance and duration; they return with new observations, ideas, attitudes, experiences, skills, and enthusiasms.

An outside visit may deepen the pupils' awareness of the world they already know, so that a familiar environment can become an exciting and stimulating field for research, or it may extend their experience by introducing them to new environments, to fresh skills, and to different social and vocational situations. Through such contact with the world outside, classroom studies acquire purpose and relevance and learning becomes meaningful.

It is repeatedly recommended that secondary-school pupils be taken on outside visits relevant to their school-leavers course. But preparation for life after leaving school is not confined to the final year; it runs through the entire period of education, and an increasing number of schools organize visits that afford opportunities for social, vocational, and environmental studies.

The value of outside visits in fostering the social and personal development of young people is widely recognized both within the schools and by such outside agencies as youth movements and voluntary organizations. It is in situations where pupils are expected to exercise responsibility and self-control that qualities of co-operation, perseverance, initiative, and self-discipline are developed. It is hoped, therefore, that the teacher organizing out-of-school activities will seek gradually to reduce the degree of constant supervision that is described in the following chapters and will lead his pupils towards self-discipline, towards a situation in which outside activities can safely be undertaken by small groups, fully briefed, equipped, and organized to conduct themselves in an effective and responsible manner.

In a publication prepared for teachers by teachers it is unnecessary to state that the value of out-of-school activities lies in their relevance to the pupil and to the curriculum: out-of-school activities form an integral part of the educational programme. Every visit should therefore be preceded by careful educational preparation. The pupils involved must know the aim of the visit, what it is intended to accomplish, and its place in the pattern of the school course. Equally important is follow-up work – the discussion, interpretation, collation, and recording which enable pupils to understand the value and significance of the visit and which stimulate further development and learning.

II. Organizing for safety

The teacher's responsibility

For many children – and some adults – the best visit is the spontaneous one, the excursion devised on impulse, according to whim or weather, in a spirit of adventure, ending at any place, any time. But the teacher in his professional capacity cannot undertake such excursions: the safety of the pupils in his charge depends on meticulous planning of every stage and aspect of the visit.

Safety, in this context, does not consist merely in the absence of accidents, but in a positive state of mental and physical security, a state that is constructively planned for by a procedure that meets all the teacher's responsibilities. The teacher is responsible

> TO   the headteacher
> the employing authority
> the parents
> FOR   the pupils in his charge.

To the headteacher

In the planning and organizing of his work in school, the teacher is directly responsible to his headteacher or principal. It follows that in planning out-of-school activities he must first seek the headteacher's approval for the proposed activity and his authority to make arrangements with the outside agencies involved.

Once the arrangements have been made, the teacher should submit to the headteacher full details of the visit planned, the proposed activities, supervisory provision, transport arrangements, and insurance cover. The headteacher can assist the teacher in fulfilling this responsibility by issuing a form of the kind reproduced on pp. 15 and 16.

To his employing authority

The educational value of school visits is widely recognized by local education authorities, many of whom have evolved specific policies regarding such visits and consequently are able to provide positive guidance for teachers undertaking them. Before planning a visit the teacher should, therefore, find out his employing authority's policy and regulations concerned with out-of-school activities. These should be obtainable from the headteacher.

The employing authority is responsible for the 'commission of acts or omissions which arise in the course of employment and which constitute negligence.' 'In the course of employment' means not only while on or about school premises, but while participating in any activity connected with duties required by or approved by the authority. In his own interests, then, the teacher will wish to ensure that the visit he plans is formally approved by the authority.

The authority, since it accepts liability, is entitled to have adequate notice of the visit and to lay down such conditions regarding number of teachers, age of group, etc., as will provide reasonable safeguards. As each authority is responsible for framing its own regulations and conditions, these will vary from one authority to another.

The majority of local education authorities do arrange adequate insurance cover for out-of-school activities, but it is wise to submit full details of the project to the authority in order to determine the extent to which the LEA's insurance cover is effective.

Teachers in charge of school journeys during holiday periods should ensure that their activities can be construed as being 'in the course of employment' and, if any doubt on this point exists, to effect specific insurance cover.

An additional insurance problem arises when school parties are

14

	DH	SM	DIRECTOR	THIS FORM TO BE COMPLETED AND PASSED TO HEADMASTER 17 CLEAR DAYS IN ADVANCE	SCHOOL VISIT	

Proposed school visit to ....   day:

                            (place)   date:

Purpose of visit:

Number of pupils: Boys.......... Girls.......... Total .... (attach list of names)

Classes involved

If in school time, will any pupils be left behind?   Yes / No   (append to list with reasons)

Names of staff accompanying pupils: (1)
                                       (2)
                                       (3)

Mode of transport:

Time and place of departure:

Time and place of return:

Recommended dress:

Reason if not school uniform:

How many pupils normally taking a school meal will not do so on account of the trip? ....

Has information sheet or worksheet been issued?   Yes / No   (attach copies)

Is first-aid box being taken?   Yes / No   (see senior master)

Have you checked on medical cases?   Yes / No

Total anticipated costs: £   *Total anticipated receipts:* £

1. Coach   Pupil contributions total:

2. Entry charge

                                (... pupils @ £ ...)

3.

4.

5.

            Total: Total:

Total subsidy requested from school fund:

(... pupils @ ... per pupil)

Please complete statement of actual costs overleaf and clear all transactions within a fortnight after the visit. Also advise headmaster of unexpected developments.

....

Teacher in charge   (date)

....

Head of department   Headmaster   (date)

Fig. 1. Form describing proposed visit

Actual costs		Actual receipts	
	£		£
1. Coach		1. . . . . . . pupils @	
2. Entry charges		2. . . . . . . pupils @	
3.		3. . . . . . . pupils @	
4.		4.	
		Sub-total A	£
		Approved subsidy	£
Total B	£	Total C	£

Notes: 1. Total in B and C should be the same.

2. Secretary to confirm receipt of amount in sub-total A less any amounts already paid and covered by receipts.

. . . .
Secretary's signature

Have you returned medical box?   Yes / No / Not taken

Report (including accident, injury, delay, difficulties)

. . . .
Teacher in charge   Headmaster

. . . .
(date)   (date)

supervised by adults other than those employed by the authority – parents, wives, or friends who offer their assistance. The authority may or may not accept liability for their actions and, again, any doubts on the matter should be resolved through the provision of additional insurance cover. In some cases written acceptance of the offer of help may enable the voluntary helpers to be covered by the authority's insurance.

Accidents may, however, occur for which no one is legally responsible, and pupils injured will have no claim for compensation unless they, or their parents, have taken out personal injury insurance.

To parents

Most parents appreciate the value of relevant out-of-school activities and many provide active encouragement individually or through PTAs. In the interests of co-operation between home and school, however, parents should always be informed in advance of any activities that involve their children being taken out of school for any appreciable period of time. The parent sending his child to school presumes that his child will be on school premises unless he is informed to the contrary. It is particularly important that parents be informed (in writing in the case of young children) when normal travelling routine to and from school may be affected. Precise details of times of departure and return must be given so that appropriate arrangements can be made for collecting or receiving the children.

Informing parents of any activity involving hazard is equally important. Some authorities require parents to sign a form of indemnity which, although it does not absolve the teacher from responsibility or exempt him from the consequences of negligence, does ensure that the parents understand the nature of the activity and the reason for it. Other authorities oppose the use of indemnity forms on the grounds that they require parents to surrender their common law rights.

For his pupils

The teacher who takes his pupils on a visit outside school knows that he bears a considerable responsibility for the safety and well-being of every member of the group. His legal liability, however, is not always so clearly understood as its interpretation may vary with circumstances. *The brief general description of the teacher's legal position given here is intended for guidance and does not purport to be definitive or exhaustive.*

17

_____ School

A journey to_____(place)

from_____(date) to_____(date) 19

I wish my son/daughter_____(name of child)
to be allowed to take part in the above-mentioned school journey and, having read the information
sheet, agree to his/her taking part in any or all of the activities described.

I understand that, while the school staff in charge of the party will take all reasonable care of the
children, they cannot necessarily be held responsible for any loss, damage, or injury suffered by
my son/daughter arising during or out of the school journey.

*My child does not suffer from any condition requiring regular treatment.

*My child suffers from_____requiring regular treatment.
(If your child suffers from a particular complaint, please enclose a letter from your own doctor
giving details of the complaint and its treatment.)

His/her National Health Service Medical Card number is_____

I consent to any **emergency** medical treatment necessary during the course of the visit.

Signature of parent_____

Date_____

*Delete where inapplicable

Fig. 2. Suggested parental consent form for an educational visit or school
journey. This form should be amended in accordance with the
varying policies of different local authorities.

Both inside and outside school, the teacher in charge of a group of pupils is deemed to be *in loco parentis*. His duty is 'to take such reasonable care of his pupils as a careful father would take of his children, having regard to all the circumstances.' In practice the law may demand a higher standard of care from a teacher than from a parent: 'The test of a reasonably prudent parent must be applied not in relation to the parent in the home, but the parent applying his mind to school life.' (Lord Justice Edmund Davies, *Lyes* v. *Middlesex County Council*, 1962)

The careful parent warns his child of danger and protects him from it. Similarly, the teacher is under a duty not to leave materials or articles lying about that are likely to injure his pupils or cause them to injure each other. The teacher is also liable when other people have left such things lying about if he knew or ought to have known of the danger and had not warned the pupils. This liability is particularly relevant to out-of-school activities, when the teacher often has little control over the environment into which he takes his pupils; his responsibility to warn pupils of possible dangers is clearly defined.

During journeys and visits outside school, the liability of the teacher does not cease at the ordinary time of the closure of the school. While he has a group in his charge, he must act at all times as a careful parent would act, irrespective of the time of school sessions. This responsibility exists not only on short visits that continue beyond normal school hours but – more significantly – on residential visits.

Preparing for safety

Successful preparation for the safety of pupils depends largely on the degree to which the teacher can foresee all the dangers and difficulties that may arise and plan to avoid or to overcome them.

Supervisory provision should be appropriate to the number in the group, the age, ability, and sex of its members, and the activities to be undertaken. Mixed groups should generally be accompanied by at least one supervisor or leader of each sex. A thorough acquaintance with all members of the group is obviously advantageous, if not essential. The teacher should know which pupils are accident-prone, which are always slow, which can accept responsibility, and which have the resilience and initiative to act promptly in an emergency.

Knowledge of the environment to be visited is equally important. The teacher should if possible make a previous visit, noting all natural and

19

human hazards and, in the case of a changing outdoor environment, the effects of weather variations.

A recall procedure is vital for most outdoor activities. The choice of procedure will be governed by the constitution of the group and the nature of the environment. The recall signal chosen may be auditory – a whistle, football rattle, or call; or visual – a flare, improvised flag, or even smoke signals! Most important is that, whatever signal is agreed, all members of the party understand its significance, rehearse the ensuing procedure, and know that prompt and implicit obedience is essential.

Rendezvous arrangements (place and time) are necessary whenever a party may become scattered. These are best made on arrival at a location so that a particular landmark can be identified in relationship to the other features of the environment. It is obvious that the landmark chosen must be unique in the locality – railway stations often have more than one clock and rural environments more than one oak tree.

A 'lost procedure' is an additional safety precaution. Every member of the group should know in advance what course of action to follow if lost – whether to stay still or to make his way back home or to a base, where to seek help or directions, whom to notify of his position or safe return.

A roll of the party should be carried by the teacher at all times so that he can make an immediate check on the presence of all its members, identify anyone missing, and speed up any necessary search procedure. If the party is to be divided into groups, separate group rolls should be issued for similar use by the appointed group leaders.

Accidents occur even in the carefully controlled environment of the school. They are at least as likely to occur to pupils on out-of-school visits. Whereas the teacher administering first aid on school premises can usually rely on additional, often expert, help, on outside visits he may have to deal alone with accidents that occur in difficult situations at considerable distance from medical facilities. For this reason a sound knowledge of first aid is essential. Some local authorities require teachers conducting out-of-school visits to hold recognized first aid qualifications, but every teacher in charge of a group of pupils must be well informed about the possible risks of injury or sudden illness and know what to do. He must be capable of undertaking:

care of wounds and control of bleeding
restoration of breathing in cases of suffocation or drowning

care of an unconscious person

restoration of the heart's action if this has stopped

care of a patient suffering from a common, acute illness such as influenza, appendicitis, food poisoning

transportation of a sick or injured person to skilled help if needed

recognition and treatment of exposure and exhaustion.

The teacher should carry first aid equipment on all visits as well as a recognized manual of first aid procedures with which he is well acquainted, so that he can refer to it with speed and accuracy. Appropriate equipment and manuals are listed in Appendices C and F. All members of the group should know before setting out what procedure is to be followed in the event of an accident.

Some of the difficulties that have been discussed may arise on any visit outside school; others may occur that have not been dealt with here. But the teacher who is prepared for all foreseeable emergencies will be more ready to deal confidently and competently with the unforeseen. With thoroughness of preparation, many anxieties can be allayed which might otherwise mar the programme, and both teacher and pupils are more likely to benefit from a safe and successful visit.

III. Travel methods

General considerations

The choice of travel method for a school visit will depend on the nature of the visit, the distance to be travelled, the cost and convenience of various methods and their availability.

Third party insurance cover is advisable for all journeys. If the group is supervised by a teacher, the third party risk will probably be covered by the LEA's public liability insurance policy, but it is also advisable for the teacher to be insured against personal liability which may not be covered by the LEA's policy. This applies equally to other adults who may accompany the group.

Times of departure and return should be stated in writing to parents. Notification of the time of return is especially important if this is after normal school hours, as parents may wish to meet their children. On road journeys, it may be convenient for children to be set down at points near their homes on the return route and parents should be informed if this is intended.

Breakdown arrangements are necessary when the return time is later than the time of school closure. If the teacher has the telephone number of the caretaker or headteacher, he can arrange for parents waiting at the school to be notified of a delayed return.

Rail travel

Reservation of compartments or coaches is essential so that the group can be kept together and supervised during the journey. On the platform station officials will advise the teacher of the stopping position of the reserved coaches. He can then assemble the children at the appropriate place and control their orderly entry into the train.

On the train unnecessary movement along corridors and gangways can be prevented by the establishment of strict toilet and buffet procedures. The teacher who knows his group well will keep overactive children and known 'fingerpokers' near him.

Accident prevention instructions should be given to the children in advance and strictly obeyed on the journey:

a   keep well away from the edges of platforms;

b   do not interfere with platform trolleys: they can cause injury and, if they run on to the line, serious accident;

c   keep away from lifts not intended for passengers;

d   never attempt to get on or off a moving train;

e   stow rack luggage with care: heavy luggage must be put in the luggage van, not in corridors;

f   do not touch door catches when the train is in motion;

g   do not lean out of windows or throw anything from them;

h   do not run along corridors or climb on seats;

i   use the handrail when walking along corridors: trains lurch and sway, particularly when travelling at speed;

j   do not carry hot liquids from the buffet car to compartments;

k   do not drink water from taps on trains unless the source is labelled 'drinking water';

l   never open doors before the train stops: they are heavy and could seriously injure or kill people on the platform;

m   in some areas stations have no recognizable platforms: be careful when alighting, and only cross the lines at authorized points.

Coach travel

The school or LEA may have a special arrangement with a local coach company. If not, however, the choice of coach company may be made on a comparison of costs, but it is as well to check that a company does not economize on safety or insurance provisions in order to lower its charges.

Reservations should be made in writing and the coach company required to confirm in writing the date, time, destination, and route details arranged.

Food and drink for the journey should be carefully planned – a ban on fizzy drinks in bottles can prevent trouble and accidents. Large cardboard boxes should be provided on the coach for food wrappings, empty containers and waste paper, and the children warned against depositing sweet papers and other litter in ashtrays.

The emergency door may have to be used in a hurry. By checking its position on entering the coach, and also the position of the first aid equipment, the teacher may save vital seconds in the event of an accident.

Travel sickness sufferers usually suffer less when seated at the front of the coach. The provision of strong paper or polythene bags and a stock of paper tissues, and the arrangement of a sickness procedure with the driver before departure, will minimize the effect of attacks. Travel sickness tablets should be administered by the teacher only with previous authorization from parents.

Windows cause fewer problems in modern air-conditioned coaches (in which they can remain closed) than in older vehicles, but the teacher should warn children against opening windows and skylights without permission. He must also ensure that children do not wave their arms out of opened windows, throw objects out, or stand up while the coach is moving.

Toilet and refreshment stops should be planned in advance in consultation with the driver. Children, especially younger ones, become very excited as the coach pulls in for such a break and need to be calmed down and instructed to walk, not run, to the café or toilet.

Double-decker journeys must be supervised by at least two teachers in order to ensure adequate control on each deck.

The following accident prevention instructions for coach travel apply equally to travel by local public bus services:

a   never attempt to get on or off a moving vehicle;
b   use handrails, especially when carrying luggage;
c   stow rack luggage carefully: heavy articles must be put in the boot or on the floor;
d   do not put your head or arms through a bus window;
e   do not throw anything from windows;
f   never run about in a moving bus or coach: a sudden stop or swerve may cause a heavy fall;
g   do not talk to the driver – except in an emergency;

h	do not pass on steps or stairs;
i	fasten belts or coats that might get caught in seats as you get off;
j	never get off a vehicle held up by traffic lights;
k	after leaving the coach or bus, wait for it to move off before you cross the road.

Local transport services

The public bus service can be used with obvious advantage for short journeys, provided that the party is small and that travel times of both outward and return journeys are well outside the rush hour. Teachers may wish to notify the transport company in advance of journeys involving more than a small group of pupils.

Discipline on buses is the responsibility of the teacher, not of the conductor. On double-decker buses it is preferable for parties of children to travel on the upper deck.

Fares should be collected from the children, if they are required to pay them, before the journey so that the teacher can pay the total amount in convenient form to the conductor and retain the tickets.

Travel by Underground

In London, travel by Underground has obvious advantages. On visits to museums or exhibitions, school parties arriving in London by rail at the main-line termini can usually reach their destination most quickly by Underground. Sightseeing tours may be conducted by a combination of Underground travel and walking, although for this purpose it might be preferable to arrange a London Transport bus tour.

Problems specific to Underground travel arise mainly from unfamiliarity with the system. The problems can be minimized by careful preparation, but special care is needed with younger children and with older pupils who have not previously travelled by Underground.

Tickets should be obtained in advance from London Transport, even for the shortest journeys, in order to avoid delay at booking offices and inconvenience to other travellers.

On escalators, one teacher should supervise pupils stepping on to the escalator in single file while another goes down the escalator with the leading pupils in order to marshal the party at the bottom away from the main traffic stream before proceeding to the appropriate platform. Although many children are now accustomed to using escalators in department stores, the length, steepness, and speed of the Underground escalators may prove unnerving.

In lifts, the party may have to travel in small groups according to the lift capacity. Each group should either be accompanied by a teacher or adequately briefed on both where to get off (if the lift has more than one stopping place), and where to wait for the remainder of the party.

On platforms, adequate control is essential. More space on the train is likely to be found at the ends of platforms than at the centre; the whole party may be assembled at one end of the platform or split into two groups assembling at both ends.

Dividing into groups may be necessary for the train journey and groups may have to travel in separate carriages or even on different trains. Such division should be planned beforehand so that each teacher knows the exact number of pupils allotted to him, and the teacher's group should be sub-divided into small groups of five or six, each with a pupil-leader. Thus on alighting from a train, for example, an instant check on numbers can be made.

Knowledge of the route and the number of stops on the journey will enable pupils travelling in a carriage without a teacher to identify each station on the carriage route map above them and to alight at the right stop. If this preparation is adequate, if reliable group leaders have been selected, if pupils stay with their group leaders at all times, and if teachers are constantly vigilant, the journey should be uneventful. However, it is useful to provide for the pupil who may fail to get off at the right stop by including in the preparatory route study the station beyond the one required. Pupils can then be told that, if they miss their station, they should get off at the next stop and move to the head of the platform to await the arrival of the teacher on a following train. By establishing this sort of procedure, the teacher can ensure that precious hours are not consumed in frantic searching and that numbers of London Transport staff are not involved in tracing 'Johnny, somewhere on the Bakerloo'.

Rush-hour travel on the Underground with school parties should always be avoided.

Cycling

Short journeys can easily be undertaken by cycle, provided that every member of the group owns a cycle, can ride it proficiently, and has parental consent to its use.

Route planning is essential so that hazardous traffic conditions are avoided if possible, and journeys should be timed to avoid rush-hour traffic. Right turns into or out of main roads are particularly difficult to negotiate and, if unavoidable, require careful advance planning.

Supervision of a cycling party is best undertaken by at least two teachers, so that one can cycle in front and one at the rear. Large numbers of cyclists may be divided into smaller groups moving separately in order to enable other road users to pass the party safely. If numbers are large, the police should be notified of the journey and their advice sought.

The Highway Code must be strictly obeyed. Pupils can usually cycle two abreast, but they must be ready to revert quickly to single file on meeting congested traffic conditions.

Other road users may be affected by a cycling party and the teacher has a responsibility to them as well as to the children in his care. He may seek their co-operation in giving way to the cyclists, but he has no authority to control traffic or pedestrians.

Walking

Crocodile formation, two abreast, although sometimes unpopular with children, is probably the safest and most effective way of organizing their movement in urban areas and should certainly be used for younger children. Older pupils in large numbers may have to be organized in crocodiles, but if numbers are small they may be allowed to walk in a staggered system in groups of two or three.

Adult supervision is desirable at both front and rear of a crocodile, but if only one teacher accompanies the group he should place responsible children at the front and rear as markers while he exercises general supervision by 'floating' along the line. The whole group must stop at every road crossing, not just the front markers, who may find themselves pushed off the pavement by those coming up behind.

Careful control is essential and instructions must be promptly obeyed by every member of the group. A stop signal, possibly a whistle, may be necessary if the party is too large or the area too noisy for a shout to be audible.

Crossing the road must be adequately supervised, especially where there is no official road crossing. Teachers have no authority to control traffic and may find it necessary in areas of heavy traffic to make previous arrangements for police assistance. Most teachers are accustomed to conducting children across the road in crocodile formation, but in a situation where this might cause a lengthy traffic hold-up, it may be preferable to use the method illustrated in Figure 3, where all the children cross simultaneously.

Other pedestrians should not be inconvenienced by the movement of the group: children usually respond readily to requests for particular care when approaching elderly or handicapped people.

On rural roads, without pavements, the Highway Code must be strictly observed. Children should move in single file at a controlled pace and should take special care at blind bends which may be approached at high speed by local drivers who are familiar with the road.

For walking in darkness and semi-darkness, light-coloured clothing or fluorescent markers are necessary, and it is advisable to carry these on daylight journeys that may be prolonged until dusk. Torches should be used at the front and rear of the party.

Mini-buses: hiring and owning

Self-drive vehicles hired for the conveyance of school parties must carry full insurance cover. If the insurance effected by the owner excludes passenger liability, the teacher hiring the vehicle must arrange additional insurance cover for this purpose.

The driver of the vehicle must also be fully covered in respect of passenger liability. This insurance arrangement can usually be made at reasonable cost at the time of booking.

A Public Service Vehicle Licence is compulsory in law for any vehicle adapted to carry eight or more passengers that carries passengers for hire or reward. Therefore, a privately owned mini-bus that carries only the normal excise licence may not be used when passengers (pupils) make any payment for the journey. If such a vehicle is used, no payment for hire or fuel may be accepted from pupils or their parents. Payment for the journey may, however, be made from a school fund on condition that no contribution to the fund by parents or pupils entitles the pupils to be carried by the vehicle. Failure to obey these regulations may render the insurance cover inoperative. The LEA insurance officer should be consulted if any doubt exists about the hiring of a mini-bus, or the purchase of such a vehicle for use on school journeys.

Crossing in file

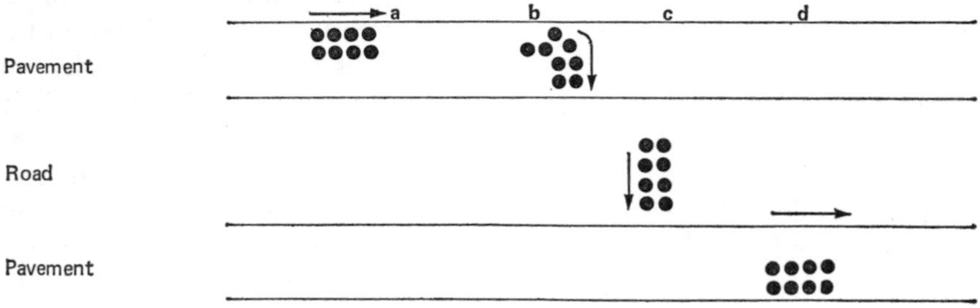

a Move along pavement
b Wait at kerb
c Cross road
d Move along pavement

In-line alternative

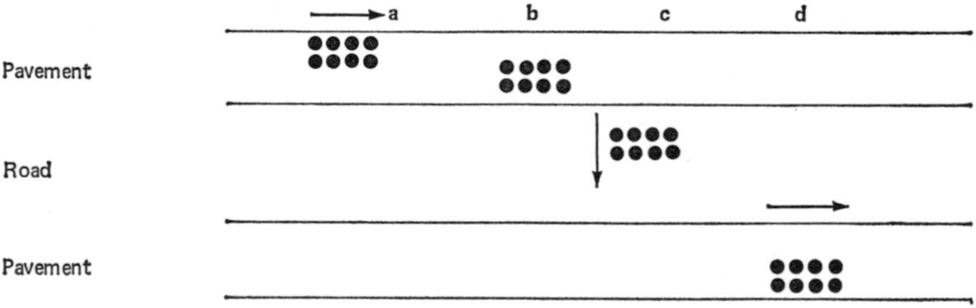

a Move along pavement
b Halt. Right turn. Wait at kerb
c Cross road in line
d Move along pavement

Fig. 3. Road crossing

29

Use of teachers' cars

The teacher's own insurance policy may restrict its cover to the use of his car for social and domestic purposes and for pleasure. If so, his use of the car on school business is excluded, and constitutes an offence under the Road Traffic Act, 1960. In accordance with the recommendations made in 1963 by a joint working party representing local authorities and teachers' organizations, most local authorities have effected Motor Contingent Liability Policies. These indemnify individual teachers in respect of their legal liability for accidents to third parties, including passengers, arising from the use of a motor vehicle in direct connexion with voluntary participation in out-of-school activities, in so far as their own insurance arrangements are insufficient for the purpose. Teachers are strongly advised to ensure, before carrying pupils in their own cars, that they are fully covered either by their own insurance policy or by that of the local authority.

Overseas journeys by land and air are considered in Chapter VII. Aerial surveys are included in Chapter IV.

IV. Day and half-day activities

Short visits out of school are the ones most commonly undertaken at all educational levels; they provide an exciting and stimulating experience for teachers as well as for their pupils. Increasing use is being made of short periods of spontaneous fieldwork, when work in a classroom breaks off and pupils go outside to observe some aspect of the environment before returning to continue their classroom study of it. Such activities form part of the normal teaching situation. Longer visits, lasting a few hours, a half-day, or a full day, demand more careful preparation. As the benefits accruing from such visits depend largely on the foresight and care with which they are organized, the notes that follow seek to guide teachers in their planning and to encourage positive thinking on the safety aspects involved.

Planning the visit

The headteacher should be consulted in the initial stages of planning. A general outline of the visit stating its purpose, its duration, and the activities proposed will enable him to assess its value to the pupils and to authorize the teacher to make the necessary arrangements. (See pp. 34–5.)

A pre-visit is desirable at this stage. The organizing teacher should visit the site or, if this is impossible, make contact with a responsible person

31

there. He needs to know the length of time necessary for the visit, the activities to be undertaken, and the facilities available – such as those for refreshment, rest, and use of toilets. A pre-visit is especially important to sites that may present particular hazards – a busy road junction at which a census is planned, an unfamiliar rural area, a farm or factory – so that adequate provision can be made for the safety of pupils.

After initial planning and a possible pre-visit, travel methods appropriate to the visit can be arranged – vehicular transport booked or routes planned for walking or cycling. The travelling time must be known so that information to parents about return time can be as accurate as possible.

The teacher should then calculate the cost of the visit, which will include transport charges, admission fees, gratuities to drivers or guides, and any other necessary payments. Many schools are able to subsidize visits from school funds, but parents usually make some contribution to the cost. If parents do contribute, arrangements can be made for regular savings and a date fixed for completion of payment. No child should be excluded from a visit because his parents are unable to meet the cost. Financial assistance for needy children may be obtainable either from a school fund or from the LEA, but it is essential that this arrangement is made tactfully so that the children concerned do not suffer embarrassment.

Staffing arrangements for supervision of the pupils will be related to the nature of the visit and to the age-range and ability of the pupils. Mixed groups should always be accompanied by at least one teacher of each sex. When an out-of-school activity extends over two or more days but does not involve overnight absence, different teachers may supervise at different times. Some local authorities lay down detailed procedures for such supervision.

LEA insurance arrangements should be examined in the context of the particular visit planned. The teacher must know what insurance protection is afforded to pupils, staff, and third parties, and whether the cover extends beyond school hours. The owners of coal mines, docks, railway premises, quarries, and other sites where special risks or hazards exist may require to be indemnified against all liabilities arising from a visit. For all visits, the LEA's public liability insurance may not in itself operate when special hazards are involved, and specific insurance protection may have to be arranged; neither will the LEA's policy necessarily relieve the teacher from his personal legal liability or protect teacher or pupils against financial loss due to accidents in respect of which there is no legal liability.

After planning is completed, the headteacher and heads of departments must be informed of the detailed plans for the visit. A suitable form for this purpose (see Figure 1, pp. 15–16) should be submitted well in advance of the visit, so that the necessary arrangements may be made within the school for school dinner numbers, staff cover for absence, and possible disruptions to games teams, choir and orchestra rehearsals, and other school activities.

Consultation with parents

Parental consent for school visits is obtained by some authorities when the children enter school. In such circumstances the headteacher may consider it unnecessary to consult parents specifically about short visits in the vicinity of the school, which in effect constitute an extension of the classroom situation. Parents should always be informed, however, of more prolonged visits and longer journeys. The information sheet circulated to them should include such details as:

> type of visit and activities planned (any activities involving special hazard must be clearly specified);
> date of visit and times of departure and return (the statement of return time is particularly important if this is later than the time of normal school closure);
> supervisory arrangements made by the school;
> approximate cost and method of payment;
> clothing and footwear required.

A form of consent should be enclosed, to be signed by the parent and returned to the school (see Figure 2, p. 18).

Preparation

Classroom preparation is essential. All pupils must know the aim and purpose of the visit, what activities are planned, and how they are to be carried out. Adequate time should be allowed for the study of background material, preparation of work sheets and questionnaires, and instruction in the use of route plans and Ordnance Survey maps of various scales. Observation will be purposeful and productive only if such preparation is thorough and the foundation is laid at this stage for sound follow-up studies.

Safety preparation consists largely of ensuring that all the pupils know the full programme of the visit and understand what is required of them at every stage. They must be warned of all known hazards, instructed in

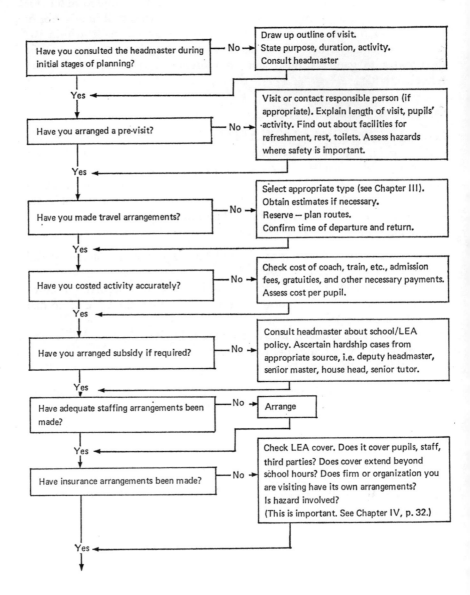

Fig. 4. Planning the project: day and half-day activities

34

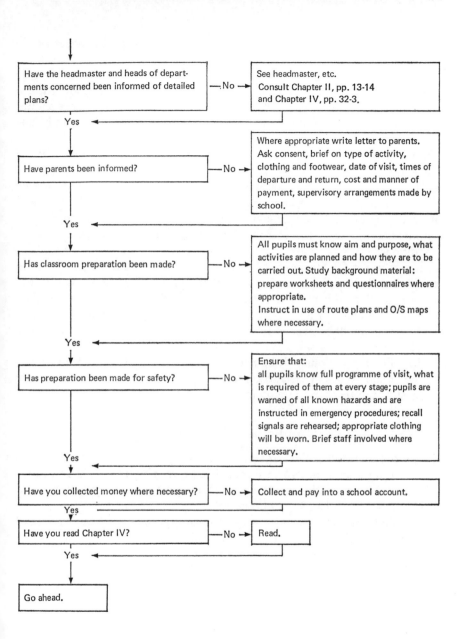

Have the headmaster and heads of departments concerned been informed of detailed plans? —No→ See headmaster, etc. Consult Chapter II, pp. 13-14 and Chapter IV, pp. 32-3.

Yes

Have parents been informed? —No→ Where appropriate write letter to parents. Ask consent, brief on type of activity, clothing and footwear, date of visit, times of departure and return, cost and manner of payment, supervisory arrangements made by school.

Yes

Has classroom preparation been made? —No→ All pupils must know aim and purpose, what activities are planned and how they are to be carried out. Study background material: prepare worksheets and questionnaires where appropriate. Instruct in use of route plans and O/S maps where necessary.

Yes

Has preparation been made for safety? —No→ Ensure that: all pupils know full programme of visit, what is required of them at every stage; pupils are warned of all known hazards and are instructed in emergency procedures; recall signals are rehearsed; appropriate clothing will be worn. Brief staff involved where necessary.

Yes

Have you collected money where necessary? —No→ Collect and pay into a school account.

Yes

Have you read Chapter IV? —No→ Read.

Yes

Go ahead.

the behaviour appropriate to each situation, and rehearsed if necessary in their response to signals of recall or emergency.

Clothing and equipment for both indoor and outdoor visits must be clearly stipulated. On 'clean' indoor visits, the wearing of school uniform is useful for identification purposes. Comfortable, low-heeled shoes should be worn for comparatively long periods of standing or walking and non-slip soles may be necessary on slippery floors in a museum or art gallery. On industrial visits, long uncontrolled hair and loose ties or belts can be dangerous near working machinery and pupils may be required to observe such site rules as those stipulating protective headgear on building sites or dark glasses while observing certain factory processes. The clothing and footwear required for outdoor visits will be those appropriate to the environment, the task, the season of the year, and the probable weather conditions.

Refreshment facilities may be available at the site of the visit or on the route, but these should be used only if the prices charged are within the means of all members of the group. If packed lunches are taken, they should not include drinks in glass bottles, which are potentially dangerous, and provision will be needed for collecting and disposing of litter after the meal.

Specific preparations will be necessary for each visit, and an indication of the various types of visits commonly undertaken by school parties may suggest to the teachers some items for consideration.

Ancient monuments and other historic buildings

Large numbers of ancient monuments are maintained by the Department of the Environment in Great Britain, ranging in period from pre-historic to seventeenth century and including cave dwellings, crosses, and bridges, as well as larger buildings.

Opening times at some sites vary according to the day of the week (and at many according to the time of year) and must therefore be checked for the date of the proposed visit.

Admission charges are levied at most buildings and sites but school parties usually qualify for concessionary rates.

Guide books, photographs, leaflets, and in some cases colour slides obtained in advance will help the teacher to make adequate preparation for the visit. Where guides are not provided, the responsibility for the way in which sites are seen and used rests with the teacher.

36

Conducted tours of great houses and castles depend for their success on the ability of their guides to communicate with children. Too often information is given unintelligibly and at great speed so that children lose interest, become bored, and misbehave. Such a situation is particularly frustrating for the teacher, who has no control over the guide but is entirely responsible for the behaviour of his pupils.

Churches and cathedrals should be visited only by prior arrangement and taking into account the times of services. Whether parties are conducted by church officials or by teachers, they should be required to conduct themselves appropriately. Permission should always be obtained for brass or stone rubbing.

Adequate rest periods and strict adherance to the time set for ending the visit will reduce the danger of fatigue. By attempting to do and see too much, children may become so tired that the visit loses value.

Archaeological work

Digs in progress are fascinating to most children, who are usually eager to join in the 'treasure-hunt'. They need to be specifically warned against disturbing or picking up fragments, against well-intentioned attempts to join in the digging without invitation, and against obstructing the diggers in their work.

Digging on archaeological sites must be undertaken only with official permission. Complaints have been made about parties of escorted young people who have dug on archaeological sites without reference to anyone except the landowner or tenant. It is the duty of any responsible leader to make contact with the local museum, archaeological organization, or other official body before digging or collecting objects and specimens.

Museums

Museum authorities should be notified in advance of party visits and arrangements should be made with the schools officer.

Classroom preparation should include establishing the purpose of the visit so that pupils know what to look for and where to look for it (with the aid of plans for large museums), preparing worksheets, questionnaires and sketches for identification, and equipping each pupil with board, paper, and two pencils.

The length of the visit depends upon the age and ability of the pupils;

walking round museums can be particularly tiring for younger pupils. For young children a stay of not more than an hour is advisable, whereas older pupils from secondary schools may profit more from a half-day visit. The teacher who knows both pupils and museums well is able to adjust the time/fatigue/interest relationship accordingly. Rest and refreshment periods effectively break up a long visit. If arrangements are made in advance, some museums provide film shows, which can be timed to prevent the onset of fatigue.

Supervision and adequate control are essential on museum visits. Children running on highly polished floors among glass cases, leaning heavily on exhibits, or rushing up and down stone staircases can cause and suffer serious accidents. Even when a schools officer or other official of the museum is lecturing to pupils or acting as guide, responsibility for discipline rests with the teacher.

Exhibitions

Morning visits to exhibitions are advisable and the number of pupils in the group should be determined by the size of the exhibition and the attendance anticipated. Fatigue can be reduced by planning the route through the exhibition area so that children do not rush aimlessly around the exhibits, by ensuring that refreshments are available, and by taking advantage of any rest opportunities offered.

Control of pupils is more easily maintained if they are wearing school uniform. The value of periodic rendezvous arrangements will depend on the nature and size of the exhibition; in some circumstances such arrangements could be too time-consuming.

The coach park of a large exhibition centre may prove bewildering and frightening to a child who is searching for his own coach among rows of seemingly identical vehicles. Before entering the exhibition, easily found meeting points can be arranged for the collection of pupils at the end of the visit, so that they can all leave the exhibition together. The establishment of a clear 'lost child' procedure is also advisable.

Retail shops

Survey work is often organized in large chain stores, department stores, supermarkets, and street markets. Permission is necessary, however, before taking groups of children into any store, however large, and advice on the best time to visit should be sought.

Preparation will include a clear statement of the purpose of the visit and the information to be sought: pupils equipped with plans or store guides will be able to find their way competently to the relevant departments. The visit should be short, allowing just sufficient time for completion of the task and no spare time for shop-wandering.

Control of the group is essential. The teacher must know his pupils sufficiently well before attempting this kind of work to be confident that they will behave responsibly and will not inconvenience traders or customers. The use of escalators should be supervised, particularly if the children are unused to them, and the operation of unattended lifts must be forbidden. Meeting points may be specified in large stores, and a time and place for meeting when the work is finished.

Urban fieldwork

The growth of environmental studies, social economics and civics courses, and the development of other outward-looking studies of the 'Newsom' type, have led to a considerable increase in the number of children going outside the school. The activities undertaken are of such variety as to defy a common planning procedure: all that is possible in a guide of this kind is to refer to some common aspects of organization.

The working area must be clearly delineated on maps of adequate scale. By walking over the area beforehand, the teacher can check obvious danger points such as main-road crossings, railway lines, unfenced canals, and derelict buildings. He must warn pupils of those dangers which are unavoidable, and exercise careful supervision: this entails keeping the group together and guarding against the temptation to stop with some pupils to answer questions or to point out details, while others walk on some way ahead.

Group assignments are often preferable in work of this nature. Groups of three or four are suggested, as a small number reduces the inconvenience to the public and minimizes the likelihood of sky-larking.

Work in unsupervised groups should be planned for short periods only. Each group will need check-points and a map showing the group's route and the teacher's route so that the teacher can be contacted promptly in an emergency. Previous noting of telephone kiosks in an unfamiliar area may save considerable time in an emergency situation.

Once a time-limit is set, pupils must assemble at the agreed time

39

whether or not their work has been completed. The time taken will vary according to the tasks set and the area of work – pupils may be working in the immediate school area for less than an hour or for longer periods in a nearby town. The party must return to the school for dismissal, unless they are working very near school premises, and on no account should the children be dismissed before official school closing time.

The movement of pupils in urban areas should not inconvenience the public. For senior pupils in moderate numbers a staggered start in groups of two or three is suggested, with adequate supervision at busy crossings where no official road crossings are available. For younger pupils a crocodile formation is preferable with reliable pupils at the front and rear (see Figure 3, p. 29).

Rural areas

A code of behaviour, clearly established and firmly adhered to, is essential to the success of day and half-day trips to the country or seaside. A previous visit to the area and local advice will enable the teacher to plan routes (noting all potential hazards, including high water times in coastal areas), to establish the scope of activity, and to determine whether pupils will work as a party or be divided into groups.

If the teacher decides upon group work, he will need to take special care in planning adult supervision. He must ensure that each group has a watch and knows the time set for the party to reassemble. In addition to the first aid equipment that the teacher will carry even on the shortest visit, he must see that group first aid kits are provided when work is planned over a large area. A recall signal appropriate to the nature and extent of the working area should be agreed, and an emergency procedure established. (Previous map study and compass work may be necessary for defining emergency procedure in open country.) Some groups may be subject to cold, wet waits for reassembly of the whole party and there is danger of exposure and exhaustion, especially in adverse weather conditions in exposed areas.

Weather conditions can change rapidly, particularly in upland and coastal areas. The sudden onset of mist or fog is a danger, while showers and storms substantially change conditions underfoot. If conditions are likely to become hazardous, the party must be kept together and protected as well as possible.

Movement over countryside should be at a controlled pace (with running prohibited), and in single file along a country lane or the side of a field. Children unused to walking long distances may become footsore and their weariness tends to be increased by an unfamiliar environment. After too long a walk, tired children may be straggling far behind the main party or struggling to catch up with it; both are potentially dangerous situations.

Private land that has no public footpaths may be crossed only with the permission of the owner and his wishes must be respected even if they appear unreasonable: no greater statutory right of access exists for school parties than for other members of the community. Strict control of the party is essential so that its members do not damage crops, fences, or stream and pond margins, disturb animals, or leave litter. If the area is left as it was found and the owner is thanked personally or by letter for allowing the visit, he will be more inclined to permit further visits.

Collecting specimens is a compulsive occupation for most children and their enthusiasm for it may have to be curbed. Briefing of group leaders and strict control can prevent the collection of unnecessary specimens – many items can be sketched or photographed instead. Permission is required for the collection of any specimens on nature reserves and on National Trust property.

The dangers of poisoning from eating berries, fungi, or sprayed crops must be clearly pointed out, particularly to children unfamiliar with rural environments.

Relaxation periods between completion of work and the return journey may be the times of greatest danger. Swimming is the obvious relaxation in coastal areas or by rivers, but this can be allowed only if parents' permission has been previously obtained, if a number of pickets appropriate to the size of the group are posted, and if a qualified life-saver is present. Lifeguard Corps members in the area may be prepared to offer their services if previously requested by the school to do so, but usually only at weekends. Darting across roads to buy ice-cream or sweets, climbing cliffs and crags, exploring caves, playing near rivers and streams are examples of what can happen in various locations. Teachers too may be tempted to relax at this stage after strenuous work, but they must be aware of the obvious dangers and be prepared to exercise continuing vigilance.

Quarries and sand and gravel pits

Permission is necessary before visiting sites and details must be obtained of blasting times and the precise areas of the quarry that the party can safely visit.

41

Clothing appropriate to the visit will be warm, windproof, and dust-proof: strong, comfortable, thick-soled shoes will be needed and protective headgear may be issued at the quarry. Hazards to guard against include dust, flying stones, and splinters of rock. Pupils must be warned in advance to keep away from workers, machinery, and lorries, to avoid climbing over loose stones and sand or gravel piles, and, if they must climb, to keep to pathways.

Hammering must be meticulously controlled to prevent the dangers of rock splinters and falling rock fragments, and no individual or group should work below another. The work must be planned so that the teacher is in a position to direct observation at all times.

Farm visits

The National Farmers Union arrange each year for thousands of school children to visit farms in England and Wales. They consider that these visits promote better understanding between town and country and they stress the importance of proper planning to the maintenance of the genuine goodwill that exists within the industry. The minimum age for NFU-sponsored visits is ten years: for younger children visits to agricultural shows will offer the opportunity to see farm animals and to gain some appreciation of farming life. A month's notice is the minimum stipulated for arranging a farm visit. Farms near urban areas and in holiday regions tend to be over-visited and teachers are asked to be flexible in negotiating visiting dates and distances to be travelled. Preliminary visits to the farm by teachers are important; the burden of repeated visits upon the farmer can be relieved if the teacher knows the farm well and has the farmer's confidence.

Preparations will include a clear statement of the purpose of the visit (to the farmer as well as to the pupils), arrangements for pupils' meals, and advice on suitable clothing and footwear. The hazards inherent in the farming situation must be clearly explained before the visit, particularly to town children who tend to regard farming as a holiday rather than as a highly mechanized industry. Delayed arrival, possibly due to travel difficulties, can seriously inconvenience a farmer who has a heavy work commitment. He should be notified if at all possible of any delay and should certainly be informed if a visit has to be cancelled. Most teachers ensure that letters of thanks are written after a visit; these both contribute towards goodwill and encourage pupils to develop standards of courtesy.

Discipline of behaviour and movement must be rigorous throughout the visit. The group should be small – a maximum of twenty pupils per teacher – and should be kept together when moving from one part of the farm to another. Loiterers tend to be 'fingerpokers' and many electrically-operated machines start easily when a button is pressed. Other potential hazards to be avoided include rakes, ladders, chemical sprays, barns, hay bales, ponds, cess-pools, tanks, wells, and all items of equipment and machinery, particularly tractors. Pupils' behaviour towards farm animals should be strictly controlled, so that no animals are inappropriately fed, petted, or goaded.

Aerial surveys

The increased use of aerial surveying has led to the establishment of relevant regulations by an increasing number of authorities. In some areas specific approval of managers, governors, or the local authority is required before organized groups of pupils are taken on air flights. LEA insurance provisions may not include cover for air travel and specific insurance arrangements may be necessary.

Route plans and flying height (usually 1000–1500 ft) will be agreed in advance with the air charter company in accordance with the teacher's requirements.

Classroom preparation will include a study of the map of the survey area and instruction in the use of a superimposed route plan, so that pupils on both sides of the plane can follow all stages of the journey.

The success of the survey can depend on weather conditions. Air charter companies seldom allow cancellation because of cloudy weather; they may, however, cancel because of fog and the school may have to accept an alternative flight date.

Community service

The development of social awareness and sound relationships with the community as a whole is now universally recognized as an integral part of the education of older children, and many schools offer opportunities for community service and social studies as well as work experience and vocational guidance projects. These schemes place a considerable responsibility on the teachers who organize and direct such activities in many differing situations. The suggestions given here for the general guidance of organizing teachers are intended to be interpreted according to the age and ability of pupils and adapted to suit the activities planned.

Arrangements for community service are often made by an organization outside the school, such as a charitable or voluntary body, a church, a hospital, or a welfare agency. The nature and extent of the work expected of the pupils must be clearly defined before any arrangements are undertaken by the school. The responsibility for pupils sent out of school to work in unsupervised groups must be clarified in writing with the head of the organizing body or with the person in charge of the institution to be visited, such as the matron of a hospital or the warden of an old people's centre.

Parents should be informed of the community work scheme, of the work their children may be expected to undertake, and of supervisory provisions. It is advisable to obtain their written consent to the scheme.

The allocation of pupils to projects requires special care: the teacher needs to know pupils very well in order to try to match temperaments to each other and to the nature of the work. Reliability is an important consideration when work such as cleaning, painting and decorating, or nursing is planned.

Unsupervised travelling to and from the place of work should be arranged only after consultation with the headteacher and LEA, who may also advise on the payment of travelling expenses.

Door-to-door coverage of a district for the purpose of collecting old clothes or conducting a sociological survey does not require police permission (which is necessary only when collection of money is proposed), but the police should be notified so that they can reassure any anxious householders who telephone them. There is a need to protect the community from bogus callers; pupils or students undertaking door-to-door visits should carry an official means of identification such as a signed letter or card – school uniform and badges are not adequate for this purpose. There is a similar need to protect the students; they should visit in pairs if possible and be instructed to telephone their base if they are in any distress or difficulty.

Charity walks

Walks on main roads create danger. They are especially dangerous in areas of heavy traffic, on roads without footpaths, and in darkness. Young people walking long distances to which they are unaccustomed become tired and footsore. As fatigue increases, careful instructions are easily forgotten and hazardous situations can be created both for the walkers and for other road users. Although schools do not normally organize these walks, many organizations are turning to these voluntary activities for fund-raising. It is doubtful whether charity walks will continue to be held as they are now, but while they do continue and while some schools may wish to undertake them, hazards can be reduced by making the following safety provisions:

Participants should be over sixteen years of age. They should wear strong, comfortable shoes or boots. Their clothing should be appropriate for the season of the year and be light coloured or light-reflecting if night walking is anticipated.

The walk must start and finish off the road, the walkers being sent off at intervals in small groups with firm instructions to obey the Highway Code, especially where there are no footpaths, and the Country Code when crossing fields.

An adequate number of supervisors should be available to 'mop up', to provide transport at check-points, and to accompany the walkers if necessary. The supervisors must take care not to obstruct other road users.

In planning the date, time, and route of the walk, the police should be consulted and their instructions followed.

V. Industrial and work-experience visits

Industrial visits of a half or full day's duration have long been undertaken in British schools. On such visits groups usually consist of ten to twenty pupils with one or two teachers. Large parties are almost invariably subdivided into groups for the purpose of the visit and it is not always possible to arrange teacher supervision for every group.

Work experience lasting several days or even one or two weeks is increasingly being arranged for small groups and for individual pupils. This development received strong encouragement in the Newsom Report: it affords valuable opportunities for pupils to gain experience of work conditions or to pursue a research project in an industrial or commercial undertaking.

The safety record of both kinds of visit is generally good. As the number of visits increases, their standards of safety and success can be maintained only if close attention is paid to the objectives of the visits, their organization, and the safety precautions necessary. The field is so vast, the range of pupils involved so great, and the objectives so varied that a heavy responsibility rests with the organizing teacher to apply the necessary general principles to the planning of each specific visit.

Objectives

The purpose of any visit must be defined before preparations are made. A school that has evolved an outward-looking policy may plan visits to show pupils that subjects taught within the school are relevant and useful in the world outside – or more precisely that the school is a part of that world rather than set apart from it. The visits may be organized to foster pupils' understanding of the community in which they live: how it functions, its material and spiritual resources, what services are available to its members – particularly those handicapped or in need – and how members of the community behave, or should behave, in relation to one another. Still other visits may be organized to enable pupils to see the realities of the world of work beyond school, its disciplines and personal relationships. Only first-hand experience can give an accurate impression of particular work, but as it is impossible for any pupil to experience more than one or two jobs, he must learn about others by seeing and listening to adults and contemporaries who have had experiences different from his own. Developing powers of observation or fostering particular skills may be the purpose of other visits. These objectives imply a high degree of participation and involvement by the pupils, probably over an extended period.

No single visit is likely to accomplish all these objectives, however; the teacher must determine the limited objectives of the particular visit and then consider the method by which they can best be achieved.

Planning the project

After the headteacher's approval to the visit has been sought and his authority obtained for making arrangements with organizations outside the school, contact with the organization to be visited may be made initially by private introduction or more probably through the local authority's careers officer. It is essential that the project is discussed with the person or persons who will actually be involved in the visit, although the sympathy of top management is of obvious advantage. The agreed aims of the visit should be established in writing so that they are clearly understood by the receiving organization as well as by the teacher, the headteacher, and the pupils. Any uncertainty of aims can lead to pupils finding themselves in unexpected and possibly hazardous situations.

Supervisory responsibility during a visit or course may rest with a member of the receiving organization. On industrial visits, large parties will probably be broken up into a number of small groups, each in the care of a well-briefed guide; on work-experience courses, one responsible person may undertake the supervision of an individual pupil or small group of pupils. In both situations, there must be complete agreement between all the parties concerned on the allocation of responsibility for supervision, for giving instructions to visitors, and for ensuring that the instructions are obeyed. These responsibilities cannot be expected to rest with a teacher who is far removed from some of his pupils, nor with the teacher and headteacher who are at school while pupils are engaged in work-experience courses. In delegating such responsibilities, however, the teacher must ensure that guides are properly briefed and that supervisors fully understand the purpose and nature of the work to be undertaken: he will also make periodic visits during work-experience courses to check the working of these arrangements.

The environment to which pupils are introduced on an industrial visit is often a dangerous one. Special hazards such as those of heat, cold, fumes, heavy machinery, falling objects, and poisonous liquids must be identified so that appropriate safety precautions can be taken. In some circumstances, it will be clear that certain areas of a factory must be out of bounds to pupils; in others it will be necessary to prohibit certain activities, to issue specific instructions, or to ensure that protective clothing is worn. A previous visit is essential to enable the teacher to note all hazards: if necessary he can then seek advice on appropriate measures from the local authority careers officer, the school medical officer, and the district inspector of factories.

The activities to be undertaken by each member of the group will be individually determined. Some pupils, such as those suffering from allergies or asthma, may be especially vulnerable to known hazards; work may be too strenuous for some individuals or may demand skills of which they are incapable. The advice of the school medical officer may be needed on the activities to be expected of individual pupils, as well as of the party as a whole.

Detailed approval can now be sought from the responsible authorities. The responsibility for ensuring the safety of pupils at all times rests nominally with the teacher in charge, but this responsibility will pass in part to the appropriate authorities if they have approved the proposals. Details of the programme should be given initially to the headteacher: he will probably seek the approval of his local education authority. The circumstances of the visit, the age-range of the pupils, the environment they

48

are to enter, or the activities planned may be such that the teacher or headteacher will consider it advisable to obtain approval also from the careers officer, the school medical officer, and the factory inspector.

Trade unions should be notified if pupils are to undertake any work, and contact with them can most usefully be made at factory level. If union representatives are consulted in advance and understand the precise aims of the project, they will almost invariably prove co-operative.

Legal restrictions also have to be considered if pupils are to work. It is contrary to the Factory Acts for any person below the statutory school-leaving age to accept employment in an industrial undertaking. 'Employment' includes participation of any kind in the work of an undertaking, whether or not it constitutes training and whether or not it is done for reward. The law also prohibits the employment of young persons below the statutory school-leaving age in undertakings of other kinds, except within the limits prescribed by Section 18 of the Children and Young Persons' Act, 1933 and byelaws made under it. (See the Administrative Memorandum 12/69, 'Work experience', issued by the Department of Education and Science to local education authorities.) In no circumstances should a pupil accept payment for work.

Insurance cover may have to be specifically arranged. Since pupils participating in work-experience schemes are not employed under a contract of service, they are not entitled to the benefit of the National Insurance (Industrial Injuries) Act in the event of injury through accident. Parents must be informed of this lack of coverage. LEA insurance cover varies from one authority to another in the extent to which it protects employees and third parties (in this case, employers) during out-of-school activities. It is essential that adequate cover be provided for all industrial visits and work-experience courses and that employers be adequately protected.

Transport arrangements may be required for party visits (see Chapter III), but small groups and individuals usually travel by public transport. If older, more responsible pupils are allowed to travel without teacher supervision, they must be given a strict definition of the conduct expected of them on the journey.

Consultation with parents

General consent may previously have been obtained from parents for a wide range of out-of-school activities, but specific approval must be obtained for a visit involving special hazards or one on which the pupil is actually to work. The letter of information sent to the parents should include details of the activities planned, the possible hazards involved, the supervisory arrangements, and the insurance provisions made.

Pupils' preparation

The purpose of the visit will be achieved only if pupils have a clear understanding of it in advance. In his preparatory work the teacher will need to explain the nature of the environment to be entered by the pupils and to tell them exactly what they will be required to do.

The safety regulations of the firm to be visited should not only be stated, but also carefully explained. Pupils who know the sources of danger and understand the reasons for safety regulations are more likely to develop a proper attitude of individual responsibility and less likely to indulge in dangerous horse-play. When arrangements have been made for the issue of protective clothing – overalls, headgear, footwear, or goggles – every pupil must appreciate why such protection is necessary and must be prepared to use it at all appropriate times. The receiving organization's accident procedure and first aid provision must be known to all visitors.

The code of conduct laid down for pupils will vary according to the nature and circumstances of each particular visit. The importance of a previous visit and of thorough consultation cannot be overemphasized – it is these that enable the organizing teacher to ensure the safety and well-being of his pupils by warning them against all hazards and establishing clear rules of conduct.

VI. Residential visits

Residential centres

Residential centres have been established by many local education authorities in areas affording opportunities for fieldwork and for physical challenge and basic adventure skills. In addition to using LEA centres, school parties frequently make use of similar facilities provided by other organizations (see Appendix B) and of accommodation available out of season on static camp sites and in boarding houses and hotels.

The educational value of residential courses is widely recognized: it is apparent in the measurable progress made by pupils who are given opportunities for intensive practice of physical skills or for extensive study of an environment under expert guidance, without interruption or distraction. The social benefits derived from this work are less obvious, but certainly no less important. Living and working together, pupils develop a higher degree of social awareness, so that by the end of a residential course many a pupil knows himself and his fellows more thoroughly than he would otherwise have done. Human relationships are tested under varying and sometimes difficult conditions and the individual becomes aware of his responsibility to and for the other members of the community. Social values are reappraised: attributes that appeared insignificant in the classroom assume importance and new leaders emerge in new social structures.

51

Safety awareness is fostered both in the social setting and in the activities of the residential centre. As families increasingly avail themselves of the recreational opportunities afforded by various centres such as those for sailing, fell-walking, rock-climbing, and pony-trekking, it becomes increasingly important to instruct children in safety measures appropriate to the outdoor environment. In this way the community as a whole may develop a greater safety awareness and the incidence of holiday accidents in outdoor activities may be reduced. When planning a residential visit, therefore, the teacher should consider this need for safety training, as well as the social and educational objectives of the course.

Planning the visit

The headteacher should be consulted on the general plan of the projected visit and notified of any special arrangements that will be necessary for adequate educational preparation. A pre-visit is obviously desirable, but if this is impossible the organizing teacher should obtain from the residential centre full information on the residential amenities available, the cost of accommodation (and any additional expenses), the provision of bedding and linen, and the type of personal clothing appropriate to the environment and season. If the course is to be organized by the centre, the teacher will also need to know what activities are proposed, what special clothing, equipment and educational preparation the activities demand, whether or not they involve special hazard, what participation is expected of teachers accompanying their pupils to the centre, and whether previous experience or qualification is necessary for such participation.

At this point transport arrangements should be made for both outward and return journeys (see Chapter III); the teacher will then be able to calculate the overall cost of the visit.

LEA policy towards residential education and the outdoor pursuits associated with it will probably be known to the teacher. He should, however, seek permission for each particular residential visit and ascertain whether the authority lays down specific regulations or conditions governing the qualification and experience of teachers supervising the proposed activities. Insurance cover may have to be especially arranged for specific activities involving hazard and for this purpose the authority must be fully informed of the nature and extent of all such activities. Financial assistance for needy pupils may be arranged with the LEA so that no pupil is barred from participating in a visit through lack of means.

52

Consultation with parents

Information to parents should include details of:

the type of course and the activities planned (clearly specifying any activities involving hazard);

the date and duration of the course, including times of departure and return;

supervisory arrangements made by both school and centre;

the approximate cost of residence and transport and the method of payment (saving arrangements, with a date fixed for completion of payment);

a suggested minimum and maximum amount of pocket money;

details of clothing and personal requirements and any special equipment required for activities (discussed at the end of this chapter);

the correct postal address of the residential centre and its telephone number;

the desirability of regular correspondence, particularly with children away from home for the first time;

visiting days and times.

A consent form (see Figure 2, p. 18) should be enclosed, to be signed by the parent and returned to the school.

Staffing the course

The selection of teachers for a residential course demands careful consideration. The number of staff needed will be related to the specific course, to the age, ability, and sex of the pupils (at least one teacher of each sex should accompany mixed groups), and to the staffing of the centre. The teachers selected should be those who have sound relationships of mutual trust, respect, and understanding with their pupils and who appreciate that their responsibility will extend beyond instructional periods into leisure time and night supervision. They should have the experience and ability to make a positive contribution to the course and to foster, through personal example, a sense of responsibility and reliability in all their pupils.

Specific qualifications may be necessary, for example in first aid, in mountain-leadership or in life-saving (see Appendix D).

Careful briefing of the selected teachers, and particularly of those undertaking residential work for the first time, is essential to the success of the

53

course. Every staff member should understand the aims and purposes of the course and know what is expected of him. He must be informed of his legal liabilities and of the protection afforded by insurance arrangements. He should know what residential accommodation is provided for the pupils and for himself, what medical facilities are available at the centre, what equipment there is for indoor and outdoor recreation during leisure periods, and what duties he is to undertake. In preparation for the course, he may be expected to acquire a working knowledge of the area of the centre, to establish local contacts if fieldwork is planned, or to participate in a scheme of theoretical and practical instruction in subjects relating to the course objectives, including conservation and safety.

Preparation

The programme of introduction to a residential course is of necessity more comprehensive than that for a day visit, since pupils have to be prepared for residence as well as for activities lasting a longer period of time.

The purpose and objectives of the course should be fully explained so that pupils understand how its practical activities are related to the school curriculum and how their experience during the course will be used in subsequent classroom studies. It is equally important that they realize the social value of the residential course: that the individual and collective effort demanded by communal living fosters a spirit of co-operation, and that shared experiences, even shared hardships, can prove rewarding and exhilarating. In this context a discussion of the balance between work and leisure in the course programme is relevant and pupils may suggest appropriate activities for leisure periods.

Thorough classroom preparation will reduce the amount of teaching necessary after arrival at the centre so that pupils may proceed with minimum delay to their practical activities. The interpretation and use of Ordnance Survey maps and compasses for navigation can be taught and practised beforehand. Route cards, assignment cards, or questionnaires prepared in advance encourage an inquiring approach to learning and make observational studies more purposeful and productive.

Practical skills related to the course may also need to be practised in advance. Expedition training may be required in preparation for mobile or static camp craft; initial practice can be undertaken in the skills necessary for hill-walking, mountaineering, orienteering, rock climbing, ski-ing, caving, and pot-holing; preparatory work in the local swimming baths may

54

be arranged for courses that include such water sports as swimming, water ski-ing, canoeing, sailing, and aqualung diving.

Safety training will embrace a thorough knowledge of safety precautions and rescue procedures. Pupils must know the distress signals, emergency alerts, and recall signals appropriate to the activities planned and understand the responses required of them. Even though they are to be accompanied by a leader with first aid qualifications, all pupils should have a working knowledge of basic first aid procedures and be competent to undertake artificial respiration, including mouth-to-mouth resuscitation.

Conservation methods and respect for the environment should also be taught before the visit and pupils will be instructed in the codes of conduct appropriate to the area of the residential centre. These may include:

the Country Code
the Highway Code
the Mountain Code
the Outdoor Studies Code
the Water Sports Code. (See Appendix E, pp. 96–7.)

Information about the centre will be eagerly sought by the pupils and the more detailed their previous knowledge of the centre, the more easily and quickly will they settle down after arrival. They should be as fully informed as possible on:

the residential accommodation and the facilities available for leisure occupations, shopping, correspondence;
the locality in which the centre is situated;
the course programme, its timetabling and organization;
the role of the resident staff and their relationship to the pupils;
centre regulations on discipline, personal behaviour, hygiene, and safety, and the reasons for their establishment;
the equipment provided at the centre, its care and maintenance;
domestic duties required of pupils.

Clothing and personal equipment lists should be compiled in writing, itemizing minimum and maximum requirements. The list that appears at the end of this chapter may be of assistance in compiling lists appropriate to particular visits.

At the centre

The allocation of accommodation on arrival can be effected speedily if several copies of accommodation lists and a plan of the centre have been prepared in advance by either the school or the centre staff.

First-night exuberance in some pupils can result in all the residents of the centre being kept awake for several hours: it is therefore as well to establish and enforce rigorous bed-time discipline on the first night, when many pupils will be fatigued by travel and excitement, even if this discipline is later relaxed.

The physical well-being of pupils is usually well provided for at educational centres. If medical or dental treatment is required by any pupils, the teacher in charge will need to remember that parents who have consented only to *emergency* treatment should be informed when such treatment is administered and should be consulted if any other treatment is proposed.

Emotional difficulties arise even among older pupils who are away from home for the first time. They may occasionally manifest themselves in bed-wetting. If a case of bed-wetting occurs, the teacher should first of all seek to alleviate the pupil's embarrassment and distress. He should try to prevent a recurrence by limiting the pupil's liquid consumption at the evening meal and by ensuring adequate toilet visits. Centres usually have rubber sheets in stock but if none are available, mattresses can be protected with polythene sheeting or large polythene bags.

Homesickness can be triggered off by the most trivial and apparently irrelevant incident and can spread as a form of hysteria. It cannot be dismissed as unimportant; for some children the emotional disturbance can be so great as to cause physical illness. Homesickness can generally be avoided by the prevention of boredom – by ensuring that pupils are at all times occupied in work or absorbed in recreational pursuits. The teacher who observes signs of a build-up of homesickness in his party may prevent its development by organizing a challenging activity or competition, an exciting game, an active treasure-hunt, or a special treat such as a bonfire, a barbecue, or a discotheque. An individual pupil suffering from homesickness can often be cured by being given a responsible task or a small privilege. If acute homesickness persists and is likely to endanger a pupil's health or to affect the well-being of the whole party and the success of the course, it is as well to consider the advisability of sending the pupil home, after notifying his parents. The child should not be allowed to travel alone.

Clothing and personal requirements for residential visits

Basic requirements for most centres will include:

> toilet requisites, including two hand towels
> sanitary towels
> night attire
> gym kit, including plimsolls
> sound footwear and several pairs of socks or stockings
> appropriate indoor clothing
> complete change of underclothing
> waterproof raincoat or anorak
> stationery and stamps
> sewing kit.

For outdoor activities:

> windproof anorak of adequate size
> woollen hat and gloves
> appropriate footwear, such as boots with Vibram soles
> several pairs of woollen socks
> woollen pullover(s)
> warm underclothing
> waterproof cagoule or equivalent.

Pupils should be advised to paste inside the lids of their suitcases a list of its contents. They can then use this as a check-list when repacking for their return home and so lessen the possibility of leaving property at the centre.

Other requirements that may be supplied by the school or the centre include a lightweight rucksack which can contain:

> spare dry clothing in a polythene bag
> first aid equipment
> torch with spare batteries and bulb, whistle and knife
> emergency food rations (sweets, chocolate) and day's lunch
> survival bag in 500 gauge polythene, or space blanket
> compass and polythene-covered map(s)
> route cards and assignment material
> small notebook and pencil
> special equipment for activities.

WOOLWICH FERRY

VII. Visits overseas

It is a tribute to the outward-looking policies of many LEAs and to the dedication and enthusiasm of teachers in their schools and colleges that large numbers of young people are taken each year on successful overseas visits, despite the complexities of planning and the difficulties and potential hazards. By their conduct, groups from this country have generally won the approval and admiration of people in the countries visited; the few groups that have caused concern through their noisiness and untidiness while abroad have usually been inefficiently organized or insufficiently supervised. It is hoped that the suggestions put forward here will serve as a guide, especially for the young or inexperienced teacher, to the organization and conduct of groups visiting other countries.

Teacher preparation for activities of this kind could obviously be included with advantage in the initial training programme of colleges and departments of education, particularly for those students specializing in the teaching of languages, physical education, and the natural sciences (including geography), who are likely to be the future organizers of overseas visits.

Official agencies such as the Central Bureau for Educational Visits and Exchanges (see p. 70), the Council of Europe, and UNESCO foster an increasing professionalism in organizing travel abroad, and the teacher inexperienced in this field is well-advised to make use of their expertise.

Clearing objectives

The first consideration should be the purpose of the visit and whether overseas travel is essential to the achievement of that purpose. Meticulous preparation is needed before a party of young people can be taken on a long journey to a country where the language, food, climate, and way of life may be unfamiliar. The leader must be prepared to accept a twenty-four-hour-a-day responsibility for members of his party. He is, therefore, wise to consider beforehand whether the purpose of the visit justifies its undertaking.

The nature of the visit – whether it is recreational or educational – should be clearly established. Recreational visits usually have to be undertaken during holiday periods, though many LEAs will concede some free days at the beginning or end of term. Visits planned as part of the educational programme, however, may take place during term time. For these educational visits, LEAs may give financial support so that no one is excluded through lack of means, and organizational assistance (even to the extent of chartering a ship for a carefully planned educational tour or of establishing twinning links to enable classes or whole schools to exchange visits).

Regular exchange arrangements are increasingly being established between schools and colleges, with obvious benefits arising from the accumulation of contacts and goodwill. Where no such arrangements exist, the visit organizer may consider whether the purpose of the visit and the educational programme underlying it could be better served through the establishment of an exchange scheme. Regular exchanges can be particularly beneficial to sixth-form pupils, to students of technical colleges, polytechnics, and universities, and to industrial trainees and apprentices when they offer opportunities not only for language study but also for work experience – secretarial, industrial, export and management. On visits of this kind students usually travel together and then disperse to live in ones or twos in family homes or guest-houses.

Opportunities for social contact with young people of the country visited and of other countries can greatly enhance the value of a visit, both educationally and socially. Consideration should be given in the initial stages of planning to the possibility of arranging accommodation to afford such opportunities.

Initial planning

The headteacher or principal must first approve the preliminary plans for the visit. The headteacher will also seek the approval of the management committee/board of governors/education committee before any commitment is made to an outside organization. LEAs vary in their regulations governing the minimum notice required for overseas visits, but teachers should be prepared, a year in advance of the visit, to submit a draft outline covering the following points:

> place to be visited
> dates of visit
> reason for the visit
> composition of the party
> supervision of the party
> cost of the visit and whether any claim is intended for financial help towards travel costs of any student or staff member
> details of insurance cover (most LEAs stipulate minimum insurance cover and are prepared to advise organizers in this matter)
> outline programme
> details of any special hazards involved, such as mountain climbing, canoeing
> method of organization – by teacher, travel agent or other body.

The composition of the party – the number of members, their age and their sex – will determine much of the subsequent organization. Some members will almost inevitably change their minds about participating; a reserve list may be established and a time-limit set, beyond which cancellation will be accepted only on adequate grounds.

Supervisory provision will be appropriate to the number and composition of the party. For a large party the organizer may be able to enlist the assistance of colleagues. When supervision is to be undertaken by other adults (wives or husbands of members of staff, parents of members of the party), their names must be submitted to the LEA so that they are recognized as duly authorized agents. They must also be named on insurance application forms.

The co-operation of parents is a prerequisite for planning the visit.

Through parents' meetings they can be informed of the project, consulted about such matters as itinerary planning, and involved in preparations. Some of them may be prepared to help in fund-raising and organizational chores, or to act as 'duly authorized escorts' to the party. When detailed plans have been established, full information will be sent to all parents and their written consent obtained to the visit and to all proposed activities including those involving hazard (see Figure 2, p. 18).

Travel organizations

The organization of the visit may be undertaken entirely by the party leader or it may be entrusted in part or in entirety to an outside agency.

Self-organized visits make heavy demands on the time of the leader and present numerous difficulties. Private air charter is usually expensive, as charter firms demand either a return load or a high fee. Travel by train, though cheaper, involves arrangements for the provision of meals en route and possibly couchette reservations (British Rail will advise on these matters). If coach travel is planned, the organizer may have to submit to police authorities in certain countries details of the composition of the party and of the route planned. On these and other aspects of organization, detailed guidance is available from the Central Bureau for Educational Visits and Exchanges, but before deciding to undertake all the organization himself, the leader may wish to consider whether the requirements of the party could equally well be met by a travel organization.

The choice of travel organization is best made on the recommendation of a known previous client. If this guidance is not available, the organizer should inform the Central Bureau of the aim and timing of the visit and the size and age of the group, and seek their advice on appropriate agencies or tour operators.

Non-profit-making organizations such as Educational Travel Ltd and the School Journey Association of London cater specifically for educational visits. Their travel programmes can offer greater contact with young people of the countries visited than those of travel agents. Or travel agents may themselves make detailed arrangements for visits (particularly for groups with specific requirements), or they may market on commission the tours offered by a tour operator. Tour operators offer packaged tours: they attract much of their educational business through direct mailing to schools, but an inexperienced teacher would be well advised to use only a well-established, reputable company.

Insurance arrangements

LEA regulations usually stipulate clearly the nature and extent of insurance cover required for overseas visits. Further advice may be sought from the travel agent, from the Central Bureau, or from teachers' professional organizations (who often refer such inquiries to the Central Bureau). All insurance for visits or journeys should be effected in the joint names of the organizer and the LEA. Insurance policies usually cover:

> death or disablement by accident of any member of the party;
> loss of or damage to personal luggage and loss of money;
> expenses necessarily incurred owing to enforced extension or curtailment of the visit or to any forced change in the planned itinerary of the journey by reason of strike, riot, or civil commotion;
> reasonable additional expenses incurred in connexion with the return home of any person in the party due to the death, serious injury, or illness of the parent or guardian, wife, husband, or child of such person.

Medical and hospital treatment are available free of charge only in Yugoslavia and in certain Scandinavian countries. Specific provision of insurance cover (not less than £500 per person) must therefore be made for reimbursement of:

> medical, surgical, nursing and other like expenses;
> expenses incurred by an organizer or other person in charge as a direct result of remaining with a sick or injured person;
> additional expenses incurred in transporting home on medical advice any sick or injured person or, in the event of death, the body or ashes of the deceased;
> expenses necessarily incurred by the parent or guardian of a sick or injured person travelling on medical advice to visit such a person.

The British India Steam Navigation Company require all persons participating in cruises arranged by them to be insured either under a scheme that the company has arranged or by a policy that provides no less cover. The scheme arranged by the company is generally considered satisfactory.

Finance

The cost of the visit can be calculated either as a basic cost plus optional or compulsory extras (such as cost of excursions), or as a total cost to include all expenses. A total cost is usually preferable.

Collection of money is best arranged on an instalment basis: some travel agents provide appropriate payment cards. The organizer should always pay all money collected into a special bank account and never, even temporarily, into his own account. It is as well to bear in mind at this early stage that a balance sheet for the visit may be required by the LEA.

Subsidies may be obtainable from the LEA for educational visits. Students in further education may receive grants through their firms from the appropriate industry training board. Privileged rates of travel may be available to some members of the party through their parents' occupations. Such members should be identified in the initial planning of the party since they cannot be counted in the total number necessary for obtaining teachers' free tickets or party reductions.

Pocket money must be collected in advance and exchanged by the teacher if the party is travelling on a collective passport. Teachers usually stipulate a fixed amount of pocket money for younger children. With older groups travelling on individual passports, organizers should advise on pocket money and know what amount each member is taking, so that embarrassment and possible heavy inter-pupil borrowing can be avoided.

An emergency float may be available from school funds. The organizer should also arrange with his bank manager to release emergency funds immediately if he is so requested by telephone or cable. Further financial protection is afforded by making at least some of the travel arrangements through an organization that has an office or agency in the country to be visited.

Passports

The types of passport available are:

Full British passport, valid 10 years, cost £5;
Visitor's passport (simplified form of above), valid 1 year, cost £1·50;
Collective passport for parties of five to fifteen members of under 18 years of age, cost £5.

(Applications to Passport Section, Foreign Office, Petty France, London SW1H 94D.)

Collective passport regulations include the following:

Each party must be accompanied by a leader travelling on a valid individual passport who will be responsible for the party during the various frontier formalities, including customs, immigration and currency controls, for keeping the party together and for retaining the collective travel document.

All persons named in the collective document must travel together to and from their destination and must remain together during their stay. In the event of a member of the party travelling on a collective travel document for young persons becoming separated from the party or being unable to travel back to his country of residence with the rest of the party for reasons beyond his control, the leader of the party must inform the local authorities and if possible the nearest British Consul. He must in any case inform the frontier authorities of the absence of any member of his party at the time of its departure. Any person not leaving with his party must, if required, obtain an individual travel document from the British Consulate authorities.

Collective travel documents for young persons shall be issued in original to the leader of the party, who should provide himself with as many copies as may be required for presentation at the frontier posts of countries to be visited.

(A list of the countries requiring the copies referred to in the last paragraph can be obtained with the passport application form.)

Identification cards (blank) are issued by the passport office for all members included in the collective passport who will be over sixteen years of age on the date of return to this country (prior notification of numbers is required). Countries to be visited, passed through, or entered on excursions must be stated when application is made for a collective passport. The passport office will then give information on the visa requirements of these countries and addresses of consulates from which visas are obtainable. Additional advice and help in obtaining visas may be sought from travel agencies or the Central Bureau.

Health

All group members must have the inoculations required by the countries to be passed through. They should also undergo a health check well before the departure date. School children may be examined by the school medical officer, college students by their own doctors. Particular note should be made of allergies and asthma. Those who suffer from travel sickness should be identified in advance and arrangements made for preventing sickness and minimizing its effects.

A first aid kit, assembled on medical advice, may be shared out for transportation by responsible members of the group and each individual group member should prepare a personal first aid kit.

Briefing the group

The itinerary of the visit, which may have been planned in consultation with parents and some of the group, should be fully explained to all group members, with discussion of the country or area to be visited and its climate. Accommodation and diet require careful and detailed description since they may differ substantially from those to which young people are accustomed and may demand considerable adjustment.

'Free time' should be defined – in terms of length and freedom – for the information of both group members and their parents. (In planning the programme the organizer will have recognized that excessive free time can constitute an invitation to mischief and misdemeanour.) Adult escorts and senior students who may act as group leaders need to know the range of their responsibilities and what free time is planned for them.

Luggage and personal effects

The amount of luggage to be carried needs to be strictly limited. Overloading causes fatigue, which in turn may lead to accidents. One suitcase is generally adequate, together with a small hold-all or shoulder-bag for carrying toilet requisites, food for the journey, and possibly a raincoat.

Clothing requirements will be governed mainly by the type of holiday and the activities planned, but the organizer will be able to advise specifically on clothing appropriate to the climate and customs of the country to be visited. He may also wish to advise on the quantity and ease of laundering of underclothing and on the need for stout, comfortable, but not new shoes for outdoor wear, slippers or sandals for indoors, towels, and toilet requirements.

School uniform may be required for school parties. Even if the uniform is inappropriate to the climate and terrain of the destination area, it can prove useful for identification on outward and return journeys and on main excursions.

E

Jewellery, transistor radios, cameras, and other valuables can cause numerous problems and the organizer will probably wish to advise on their carrying, wearing, and safe-keeping.

Communication arrangements

At home, duplicated copies of a communication information sheet should be left with the headteacher or principal and with the parents of group members. This will include details of:

> travel methods and times
> the full address and telephone number of the group's accommodation abroad
> the names of responsible adults in the party
> details of return home.

Abroad, the teacher will need:

> addresses and telephone numbers of parents or guardians (including holiday addresses)
> the home address and telephone number of the headteacher
> postcards, previously addressed and written, to be signed and posted on safe arrival
> several copies of the nominal roll of the party, for use at hotels and hostels or wherever the party is staying.

The outward journey

Initial assembly will have been carefully planned to allow adequate room for send-off parties and time for late arrivals. As soon as the whole party is assembled, a check can be made on:

> travel documents
> money
> luggage (correctly labelled)
> travel sickness tablets (taken and carried).

Members of the group must remember that on leaving the home area they assume the responsibility of representing their country. Every member must be aware of this responsibility and of the need for a high standard of behaviour. Supervising adults should encourage tidiness and the collection of litter in bins or boxes; throwing litter through coach or carriage windows is in some countries illegal and at all times dangerous. The group should always respect the rights of other travellers and their need for comfort and quiet.

Group travel necessitates keeping the whole group together at all times. A dispersed party makes the distribution of landing tickets on a cross-channel steamer or *contremarques* on a train difficult for the leader and can cause serious delay. (A *contremarque* is an individual's token of inclusion in the collective travel document held by the party leader and its loss may necessitate additional payment; many leaders issue *contremarques* for checking by the ticket-inspector and then collect them again for safe-keeping.) Luggage should be stowed so as to allow access to clothing needed en route – for example extra garments, raincoat, or windproof anorak for a cold Channel crossing.

Meals en route are readily arranged by most travel agencies. If pre-packed meals are taken, extra vigilance is needed to ensure the collection of litter.

Overnight travel by train can be comfortable if couchettes have been reserved: without couchettes it can be uncomfortable and difficult.

At the holiday centre

On arrival, room allocation or introduction to host families can be effected speedily if details of accommodation have been arranged in advance with a travel agency or the receiving organization. When a mixed group is staying at a centre, specific toilets and bathrooms should, if possible, be allotted to each sex and to leaders.

Arrival notification postcards must be signed and posted home as soon as possible, and the leader should check at this stage and at frequent intervals during the visit that every member of the group always carries the full address and telephone number of the centre.

Residential regulations will be established according to prior consultation with headteacher and parents and discussion with the centre management. Drinking and smoking rules may further be determined by legal requirements in the country visited. 'Lights out' rules must be enforced and a ban imposed on nocturnal activities such as midnight meals and dormitory raids which can lead to accident and embarrassment and so jeopardize the well-being of the group. If the party is sharing a centre, it must respect the privacy and comfort of other residents; it may be possible to arrange with the centre management for a special room to be allocated to the party.

Food should cause little difficulty if it has been adequately discussed beforehand, but many centres will be prepared, if necessary, to make minor menu adjustments for the benefit of a group. Packed lunches and early breakfasts before excursions and final departure are usually available if adequate notice (twenty-four hours) is given.

Health should be checked regularly; it can be affected by travelling and by climatic and dietetic changes. Early diagnosis of homesickness can prevent its spreading and jeopardizing the entire visit.

Pocket money supervision will vary with the age range of the party. With younger children it should be held by the adults in charge and rationed out daily. Older pupils may control their own money but may nevertheless welcome the opportunity to lodge large sums of money, travellers cheques, and valuables in safe keeping.

Going out from the centre

Traffic regulations and travelling speeds may differ considerably from those to which the party is accustomed – adequate warning is important.

Active pursuits, such as hill climbing, canoeing, and swimming demand extra preparation by the leader and special vigilance at all times. Chapter VIII deals with activities in hazardous environments in this country; if such activities are to be undertaken abroad, extra advice on the local regulations should be obtained in advance from the travel agent or from the Central Bureau for Educational Visits and Exchanges.

Language problems are fewer when a party is staying together at a centre, especially if one of the purposes of the visit is to increase conversational fluency. Members of a party living with families, however, may find their command of the language inadequate to meet the demands made of it and may suffer unhappiness, frustration, and homesickness. In these circumstances the party leaders must make regular visits to check that all is well. It is inadvisable for any group or party to travel abroad without at least one person who can speak the language needed; travel agencies will arrange courier accompaniment if necessary.

Advice may be needed on clothing suitable to climatic conditions – with emphasis on the dangers of overexposure when sunbathing – and to local customs. Teenage girls and young women accustomed to considerable

68

freedom of dress and behaviour in this country may, for instance, find such freedom misinterpreted by young men abroad and should, perhaps, be warned not to encourage undesirable attentions.

Practice in the use of the local currency will be useful in shopping. An experienced leader will recognize the need to steer his party away from wharf-side and street salesmen whose prices are often higher than those in a main shopping area, as well as from expensive stores and tawdry souvenir shops. Leaders' advice will probably be sought on suitable presents for families and friends; a suggestion list of appropriate, inexpensive gifts may prove helpful. A 'what-not-to-buy' list will include such dangerous articles as pointed walking-sticks and such items as flick-knives forbidden by Customs. Before shopping, the leader may wish to remind all members of the party that they must prepare a list to present to customs on return of all articles acquired abroad and that expensive items such as cameras and watches will attract heavy duty.

The return journey

A good night's sleep is advisable before the homeward journey and appeals for a last night's fling will be resisted by a wise leader.

Assembly for return is usually straightforward: checks should be made to ensure that luggage is labelled with the home address, that rooms are cleared and room keys handed in, that all property has been collected from safe deposit, and that travel documents are readily accessible. A forwarding address for any mail that may arrive after departure of the party will be required by the centre management; it is more helpful to leave a large, addressed envelope.

Passage through customs on arrival in the United Kingdom will be more speedily accomplished if members of the party are kept together and are properly prepared to comply with customs requirements. Copies of HM Customs Regulations are obtainable from any travel agency. The following points are particularly relevant:

  all items purchased or received as gifts while abroad should be listed and their value stated;

  persons under 17 years of age are not eligible for a duty free allowance of alcohol or tobacco;

  cameras and watches bought abroad must be declared and duty paid;

  if expensive foreign-made cameras or watches previously purchased in

this country are taken out during the visit, receipts or other proof of purchase may be required on return;
the importation of flick-knives is strictly prohibited.

The follow-up

School or college authorities may need a written report, and parents must be informed of any untoward occurrence. The education authority may require a balance sheet; even if this is not demanded, it is as well to prepare a financial statement and to deposit it with the headteacher or principal.

Educational follow-up in the classroom may extend over a considerable period of time: its value in reinforcing and developing the experiences gained on the visit cannot be overemphasized. Photographic displays and films will provide a valuable record of the visit and may be of interest and benefit to other members of the school or college. An evening exhibition for parents and members of the education committee is of obvious advantage.

Central Bureau for Educational Visits and Exchanges

The Central Bureau, at 43 Dorset Street, London W1H 3FN, performs two main functions. It is the national office for information and advice covering all forms of educational exchange and school, youth, and student travel. Also it is the administering authority for certain official interchange and exchange schemes. It has a number of subsidiary functions, but its basic work remains that of bringing British young people and adults into personal contact with their counterparts abroad and with life and institutions in other countries. An important consequence of this work has been the development of Central Bureau co-operation with foreign ministries, organizations, schools, institutions, teachers, and youth leaders wishing to establish exchange programmes or contact with their opposite numbers in Britain. Its work on travel, exchange, and interchange which covers pupils, students, non-student youth, teachers, and those in adult education, is distinct from that of the British Council and complementary to it, close liaison being maintained between the Bureau and the Council. It is an issuing authority for the Council of Europe's Cultural Identity Card.

VIII. Hazardous activities

Hazardous environments

Environments are influenced by many factors other than fixed geographical characteristics, which in themselves can be most formidable. Weather conditions, including seasonal variations, changes in temperature, in wind strength and direction, and in the amount of rainfall can drastically alter the nature of a locality and create additional hazards.

Mountain and moorland areas, coastal and inland waters attract young people seeking challenge and adventure, and these are areas of major hazard. They are also the areas where accidents most frequently occur, through inadequate leadership, underestimation of hazards and difficulties, inappropriate clothing and equipment, or lack of preparation.

Adequate leadership is the first essential for all parties undertaking activities in hazardous environments. Many LEAs issue regulations governing leadership qualification and teacher–pupil ratio, and teachers are advised to consult their own LEA before planning any activities in hazardous environments.

Specific qualifications and experience are necessary for the organization of activities that are hazardous. Training courses are organized by colleges and departments of education, by LEAs, by the Central Council of

Physical Recreation, and by other organizations leading to qualifications in mountaineering and rock climbing, ski-ing, winter activities, water ski-ing, subaqua diving, sailing, canoeing, and other water sports (see Appendix D). It is assumed that no teacher or leader will undertake any of these activities in his professional capacity without adequate training, specialist qualification, and relevant experience.

Preparation is necessary for all out-of-school activities: it is even more important when a party of pupils is to be taken into an area of natural hazard. The teacher should ensure that all pupils understand the purpose, nature, and duration of the proposed activity and realize what is expected of them individually and as group members. The preparatory programme will include instruction and practice in the necessary skills, identification of risks and hazards, training in emergency procedures, and study of the codes of conduct appropriate to the environment (see Appendix E).

Insurance cover should be afforded by the LEA policy for travel and activity in hazardous areas, but it is important to check that both pupils and teacher are fully protected for the specific environment and activity planned.

Parents must be fully informed of the nature of the environment, the activities to be undertaken, the dangers involved, and the supervisory provisions made before being required to give their written consent.

Mountain and upland moorland

Adventure pursuits and field studies have attracted many thousands of young people into the wilder and more remote districts of Britain. These areas are frequently beset with unsuspected hazards and present special problems for those coming from totally different environments. The teacher who wishes to take a party of pupils into such an area must ensure that both he and they are competent, adequately prepared, and fully equipped for the environment and the activities to be undertaken. The project should be planned so as to be well within the teacher's previous range of experience and should preferably be undertaken in country familiar to him. In some local authorities possession of the Mountain Leadership Certificate is required of teachers taking pupils to remote upland moors and mountains exceeding 2000 ft in height; it is desirable for all teachers organizing activities in upland areas.

The structure of the party will be determined by the nature of the activities planned. In field studies, pupils are usually taken to the study area as an entire party and divided into smaller groups for observational

72

work; in adventure pursuits group organization may be used throughout a project. In both situations groups should consist of at least four, preferably five members for safety. Group leaders should be selected with care, since responsibility and authority will devolve on them and all group members must have confidence in their leadership. Each leader must know the capabilities of his group and realize that its pace and endurance are governed by those of its weakest member.

The safety and efficiency of parties will depend on the undertaking of a comprehensive programme of preparation, with particular reference to:

route preparation
navigation
weather conditions
emergency procedures
clothing and equipment.

Route preparation

Every member of the group must have adequate knowledge of the activity area, including known safe routes, escape routes, and all route hazards such as exposed ridges and precipices. Route planning must take into account the type of country, the distances and heights involved, and the nature of the activity in relation to the capabilities of members of the group. Rates of travel must also be considered in route planning. Normal walking rates are as follows:

in good weather – on level tracks	$2\frac{1}{2}$–3 mph
over rough ground	2–$2\frac{1}{2}$ mph
against force 7 or 8 wind	$1\frac{1}{2}$–2 mph
in deep snow	1–2 mph

Naismith's Rule for calculating pace under full load in mountainous country is:

'Allow one hour for every $2\frac{1}{2}$ miles as measured on the map.
Add 1 hour for every 1500 ft climbed.' (See Figure 5.)

Route cards (see Figure 6) will show the route planned (with possible alternative routes in bad weather conditions), details of check-points, and time of return. When setting out, the leader should ensure that a copy of the route plan, including alternative routes, is lodged with a responsible person or left displayed in a prominent position.

73

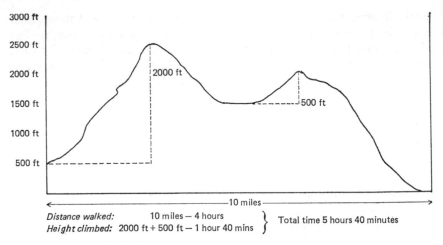

Distance walked: 10 miles — 4 hours
Height climbed: 2000 ft + 500 ft — 1 hour 40 mins } Total time 5 hours 40 minutes

Fig. 5. Naismith's Rule

Navigation

Good navigation in wild and hilly country rests on more than a theoretical understanding of techniques – it requires map craft; height gained must be conserved and routes should avoid difficult terrain whenever possible. Practical interpretation of map and compass must, therefore, be undertaken in field conditions where the basic skills of map craft can be seen to have direct relevance to navigation. Efficient map reading involves identification of landmarks, interpretation of landforms in terms of relief and height, estimation of distances, compass navigation, and orientation of maps. Preliminary training in these skills should aim to impart interest in map craft as well as theoretical knowledge.

Weather conditions

Preparation must be made for all weather conditions. Despite the obvious precautions of noting weather forecasts (particularly warnings of gales, frost and snow, or hill fog) and obtaining sound local advice in areas where high altitude conditions may differ from those on the valley floor, groups may meet hazardous conditions caused by sudden weather changes. Particular hazards are:

    wind and snow combining to form blizzards

ROUTE CARD

Group	Leader:_____	Date(s)
	Names of students_____	
	_____ _____	Duration:
No. in group:	_____ _____	_____Hours
		_____Days

Type of activity	Camping expedition		Field studies		Rock climbing	
	Canoeing		Hill walking		Sailing	
	Caving		Orienteering		Swimming	

ROUTE PLAN   Ordnance Survey Map(s)
_____

| FROM: | Location | Grid reference | TO: | Location | | Grid reference |

FROM	TO	DISTANCE	HEIGHT	TIME

Alternative arrangements.

Transport arrangements	OUT	IN
	Dropping point_____	Pick up point _____
	Time _____	Time _____
Checked by:		

Fig. 6. Route card and route plan

heavy rainfall swelling streams and extending bogland and marsh
dense mists and hill fog
electrical storms affecting ridges and summits.

On meeting such conditions, groups must be prepared to:

    a return to base
or **b** descend by the safest route, to a known refuge if possible
or **c** set up an emergency bivouac when necessary. (Instruction should be given in setting up the bivouac in particular conditions such as snow or electrical storms.)

Emergency procedures

All members of the group must know the International Distress Signal:

International Distress Signal
1. *Six* whistle blasts (or six shouts or flashes of a torch or waves of a light-coloured cloth) at 10-second intervals
2. one minute's pause
3. another six blasts at 10-second intervals.

Answering signal
1. *Three* blasts at 20-second intervals
2. one minute's pause
3. another three blasts at 20-second intervals.

Competence in simple first aid is necessary. It should be understood, however, that treatment must be limited to the knowledge and experience of the group.

    Emergency procedures must be established and understood. Instructions might include:

If a party is lost, its members must keep together.
If benighted, they must shelter from the wind, put on all spare clothing and huddle together for warmth.
If someone is injured, he must be kept warm and comfortable and well-tended by his companions.
If assistance is necessary, *two* persons should be sent – well-clad, warm, and sustained by easily-assimilated food. They must mark the

---

accident position on the ground and on the map, note their route to the rescue post, and, on arrival, give precise details of:

    position of casualty
    time and nature of accident
    number of persons involved
    type of assistance required
    medical assistance required
    return route.

Exposure and exhaustion may occur in wet, cold conditions and all members of the party should know the symptoms and what immediate treatment is necessary.

Signs and symptoms of exposure
    complaint of tiredness and cold, lack of interest
    strange and unreasonable behaviour
    slurred speech and violent outbursts
    slowing down, stumbling, falling frequently
    blurred or disturbed vision
    collapse and unconsciousness.

Immediate treatment
1. insulate as quickly as possible against further heat loss:
    put in dry sleeping bag, with additional coverings for head and face as well as body
    place a companion alongside to give body heat
    shelter from wind and rain
    insulate with plastic raincoats, ground sheets, or polythene bags;
2. give sugar in the most digestible form available – powdered glucose, sweets, condensed milk, hot sweet tea;
3. apply mouth-to-mouth resuscitation if respiration has ceased and continue until its resumption.

Clothing and equipment

Advance planning and inspection of clothing and equipment is necessary. Last-minute failure to include an essential item may jeopardize the safety of an individual and of the whole group.

For hill walking, for example, each individual will need:

77

boots that provide a firm grip on wet or slippery surfaces

several pairs of comfortably-fitting, woollen socks

windproof anorak or cagoule, preferably brightly-coloured for identification of position

warm gloves – woollen or nylon fur

close-fitting headwear

spare clothing for emergency use, including pullover, gloves, trousers, socks

blanket or survival bag (a 6 ft × 3 ft bag of 500-gauge polythene is cheap and effective)

torch, whistle, and knife

food – emergency food rations as well as day's lunch

compass and polythene-covered map(s)

route cards and assignment material.

For mobile camping and expedition work, guidance on clothing and equipment is given in the DES Education Pamphlet No. 58, *Camping* (HMSO, 1971), and in other publications listed in Appendix F. Load carrying must be carefully controlled. No individual should carry in excess of 35 lb, and a much lower weight is desirable; this can be achieved without impairing efficiency, through careful planning and selection of equipment.

Caves, pot-holes, and old mine-workings

Special hazards created by weather, physical exhaustion, and nervous strain demand obedience to a rigid code of behaviour in visiting caves, pot-holes, and disused mines. To schoolchildren and teenagers in particular these locations offer challenge and fascination, but they must be warned of possible dangers and required to take basic precautions. Minor accidents, for example falling, are the most common hazard and may require a complicated rescue operation.

Clothing

Most underground 'incidents' involve the problem of exposure, the loss of heat from the body. Victims rarely die from their injuries, more commonly from exposure. The choice of the right clothing to conserve heat and energy is therefore essential. Experienced cavers wear 'wet-suits' of Neoprene but these are expensive. The cave explorer should, however, wear at least two layers of clothing with wool next to the skin, preferably covered by a

78

one-piece overall. The legs must not be forgotten – grandfather's long combinations serve admirably!

A protective helmet with chinstrap is essential, and footwear should consist of climbing boots with well-serrated rubber soles. If wire ladders are to be climbed, hooks on the boots for lacing purposes are dangerous, as these tend to hook themselves on to the wire and are difficult to release. Rubber-soled boots may well be a disadvantage on wet limestone on the surface, but below the surface, where conditions may be different, rubber soles are suitable, although it would be better to avoid the use of wellington boots in all cases.

Equipment

Lamps are of paramount importance and must, therefore, be of excellent quality. They should be robust, waterproof, and of proven lighting capacity and reliability. Lead–acid accumulators or 'miner's lamps', although expensive initially, fit this description and prove economical in the long term. Acetylene lamps are useful in dry caves but care has to be taken when using them in conjunction with nylon ropes and in wet conditions. Many will be tempted to rely upon bicycle lamps, attractive because of their cheapness and availability, but their use must be discouraged; they are unreliable and therefore unsuitable. Whatever type of lamp is used it should be firmly fixed to the helmet and NOT carried in the hand. Appropriate spares and, if possible, alternative lighting (even candles or matches) should be carried.

Climbing equipment (ladders, ropes, etc.) is of a specialized nature and requires expert advice in use, choice, and maintenance.

Food should be carried by all parties. High-energy, protein foods are most satisfactory; raisins, chocolate, and mint cake provide good iron rations. A tube of condensed milk is an easily carried emergency food supply.

Exploration

Each party must have an experienced leader who will ensure that his party is suitably prepared for the trip and that a message is left with a reliable person (for example, a local farmer), reporting the party's plans.

Notice must be taken of the weather. Water is possibly the greatest hazard, and a heavy rainfall can cause a cave to flood with disastrous rapidity. Forgetting the demands of the return journey is a frequent cause of trouble, particularly in pot-holes with ladder climbs. The hardest part of caving is the return. Allow, therefore, 'two hours out for one hour in'.

The exploration of old mines should not be undertaken lightly by the experienced or at all by the inexperienced. These additional precautions are necessary in old mineworkings:

> Although explosive gases are rare, CO_2 is not. It is odourless and a killer. Therefore some means of detection (a candle, for example) must be carried.

> Many shafts and passages are propped by timber emplaced 200 years ago. Therefore extreme caution is required.

> Miners' waste may form false floors and roofs. A shout may dislodge them.

> Mineworkings often form a bewildering maze of passages and the incautious can easily become lost. It is as well to ensure that the return route is well marked.

Field parties will come across caves and mineworkings in many areas of upland Britain. While admitting their value as sites of educational interest, it is inadvisable to explore such places without experienced leadership. Such leadership can often be found in local caving clubs who are usually prepared to assist genuinely interested people.

Exposure is also a danger in caving. All members of the party should be able to recognize the symptoms of exposure, know what emergency action to take, and how to contact the rescue service if necessary (see p. 76).

Coastal and inland waters

The danger of drowning during field study work near a river, canal, or lake, or at the seashore, while not always apparent, is none the less present. A child's swimming ability in cold muddy water is considerably less than in a heated swimming pool, and an accident in any depth of water can prove fatal unless prompt action is taken. The teacher planning activities in or near water should, therefore, ensure that either he or a responsible member of the party has training and experience in life-saving and in techniques of artificial respiration, including mouth-to-mouth resuscitation.

Tidal dangers can be largely avoided by planning visits in accordance with tide tables. These are published annually by the British Transport Docks Board and can be obtained through a local docks office. But tides do not always adhere strictly to the tide tables; a high tide may be higher and earlier than forecast, and a safety margin should, therefore, be allowed in the time schedule. Schools should also consult the appropriate river authority before undertaking expeditions on rivers.

Cliffs may be unstable due to erosion and undercutting. If passage immediately below them is unavoidable, it should be effected as speedily as possible and pupils should be warned of the danger of head injury through falling rocks and stones. Cliff climbing is exceedingly dangerous in any circumstances. Cliff-top walking must be strictly controlled and pupils specifically forbidden to approach the cliff edge, even if dared to do so. All 'dare' games are to be avoided, including Canute-like activities at the sea's edge.

Recreational activities on the beach may be the main purpose of the visit (games coaching is often undertaken on wide stretches of sand), or they may follow a period of field study. If pupils are likely to become scattered during the course of such activities, a time limit should be set and a recall signal agreed and understood.

Rowing boats, canoes, and pedaloes may be available for hire on popular beaches. As their owners seldom ascertain a child's ability to swim or to handle a boat, the teacher must assume full responsibility for the activity and insist on appropriate safety conditions such as swimming ability, use of life jackets, and operating limits.

Sea bathing should be undertaken only in suitable conditions and under the supervision of an adult holding a Bronze Medallion, a Life Guard Proficiency Award from the Royal Life Saving Society, or a Surf Bronze Medallion from the Surf Life Saving Association of Great Britain.

Before allowing bathing the teacher should know the local hazards, tidal conditions, rip tides, depth of water, and current. He must determine, according to tidal flow, the bathing area and the direction of swimming – whether outwards to a marker buoy, for example, or parallel to the beach. (Although tidal waters appear to flow towards and away from the beach, the actual flow is parallel to the beach except during 'slack' water at high and low tide.)

In planning the activity the teacher should aim to develop confidence and foster enjoyment in a safe situation, bearing in mind that swimming ability acquired in a heated swimming pool is considerably reduced in the sea by heavy waves, low temperature, and undertow, and that children are often unsure of their balance and easily knocked over by waves; they may need time and help to overcome fear.

Safety precautions must be explained to all pupils before they enter the water. A recall signal (usually a whistle blast) must be established, understood, and obeyed. The number in the sea at any one time should be no more than can be adequately supervised. Pupils should be counted on entering and leaving the sea and during the course of the activity. The use of a pair system ensures that no pupil is left entirely alone.

Life-saving facilities, such as the following, should be available on the beach:

> a line and reel (details from the Surf Life Saving Association of Great Britain or RLSS)
> a rescue torpedo buoy (available as above)
> a pulling or power boat, depending on normal tidal conditions
> signal flags to direct swimmers who may be unable to hear a whistle blast (signals obtainable in simple chart form from the Surf Life Saving Association of Great Britain).

Water sports should be organized only by teachers appropriately qualified through a recognized course of training (see Appendix D). Training courses will of necessity be concerned mainly with basic principles and with the acquisition of skills and instruction techniques. Local knowledge of features such as weirs, mud flats, and sandbanks, and personal experience of the particular stretch of water at different seasons of the year, are also necessary before introducing pupils to water sports.

Participants in any water sport activity must meet the minimum requirements specified by the appropriate training manual – in swimming ability, artificial respiration techniques, and personal survival skills. Teachers are advised to check pupils' competence through practical tests in the conditions likely to be encountered during the activity. Supervision of these activities demands a high teacher–pupil ratio. It cannot be undertaken only from the shore or riverbank – at least one supervisor should be on the water to issue instructions and to ensure safety.

Safety in water sports is best ensured through strict adherence to the codes of conduct laid down in the DES Safety Series No. 1, *Safety in Outdoor Pursuits* (HMSO, 1972), chapter 2, and other relevant training manuals published by governing bodies of sport (see Appendix D).

Appendices

Appendix A Directory of addresses

A

Air Education and Recreational
Organisation
17 Warwick Avenue
Cuffley, Herts

Amateur Rowing Association
160 Great Portland Street
London W1N 5TB

Amateur Swimming Association
Acorn House
314 Grays Inn Road
London WC1

Association of Boys' Clubs
17 Bedford Square
London WC1

Association of Girls' Clubs
17 Bedford Square
London WC1

Association of Sail Training
Organisations
5 Buckingham Gate
London SW1

Association for Science Education
College Lane
Hatfield, Herts

Association of Wardens of Mountain
Centres
Aberglaslyn Hall
Beddgelert, Caernarvonshire

B

British Association of Caving
Instructors
5 St Pauls Street
Leeds

British Canoe Union (Room 315)
26 Park Crescent
London W1N 4DT

British Cycling Federation
Rooms 319/20, 26 Park Crescent
London W1N 4BJ

British Gliding Association
Royal Aero Club Aviation Centre
Artillery Mansions
75 Victoria Street
London SW1

British Horse Society
The National Equestrian Centre
Stoneleigh, Kenilworth, Warwicks

British India Steam Navigation Co. Ltd
P. & O. Building
Leadenhall Street
London EC3

British Mountaineering Council
(Room 314)
26 Park Crescent
London W1N 4EE

British Orienteering Federation
3 Glenfinlas Street
Edinburgh 3

British Red Cross Society
14 Grosvenor Crescent
London SW1

British Schools Canoeing Association
c/o Education Department
County Hall
Glenfield
Leicester LE3 8RF

British Sub Aqua Club
160 Great Portland Street
London W1N 5TB

British Transport Docks Board
Melbury House, Melbury Terrace
London NW1

British Travel Association
64 St James' Street
London SW1

British Waterways Board
Willow Grange, Church Road
Watford, Herts.

British Water Ski Federation
22 Station Approach
Virginia Water, Surrey

C

Camping Club of Great Britain and
Ireland
11 Lower Grosvenor Place
London SW1

Central Bureau for Educational Visits
and Exchanges
43 Dorset Street
London W1H 3FN

Commons, Open Spaces
and Footpaths Preservation Society
166 Shaftesbury Avenue
London WC2

Council for British Archaeology
8 St Andrew's Place
London NW1

Council for Environmental Education
26 Bedford Square
London WC1B 3HO

Council for Nature
Zoological Gardens, Regent's Park
London NW1

Countryside Commission
1 Cambridge Gate, Regent's Park
London NW1

Country-wide Holidays Association
Birch Heys, Cromwell Range
Manchester M14 6HU

County Naturalists and
Conservation Trusts
The Manor House
Alford, Lincolnshire

Cyclists' Touring Club
Cotterell House, 69 Meadrow
Godalming, Surrey

D

Department of Education and Science
Elizabeth House
York Road
London SE1 7PH

Department of Trade
(HM Coastguard)
1 Victoria Street
London SW1

Docks & Harbour Authorities
Association
3/5 Queen Square
London WC1N 3HR

Duke of Edinburgh's Award
2 Old Queen Street
London SW1

E

Educational Travel Ltd
236 South Norwood Hill
London SE25 6AZ

English Schools Swimming
Association
190 Nether Street
London N3

F

Field Studies Council
9 Devereux Court
London WC2R 3JR

Forestry Commission
25 Savile Row
London W1

G

Geographical Association
343 Fulwood Road
Sheffield 10

Geologists' Association
278 Fir Tree Road
Epsom, Surrey

Girl Guides' Association
17–19 Buckingham Palace Road
London SW1

H

Historical Association
59a Kensington Park Road
London SE11

Holiday Fellowship Ltd
Fellowship House
142 Great North Way
Hendon, London NW4

I

Inland Waterways Association
114 Regents Park Road
London NW1

M

Medical Commission on Accident
Prevention
50 Old Brompton Road
London SW7

Methodist Guild Holidays
2 Chester House, Pages Lane
Muswell Hill, London N10

Mountaineering Association
102a Westbourne Grove
London W2

Mountain Rescue Committee
Dean Hill, Wilmslow Road
Woodford, Stockport, Cheshire

Museums Association
87 Charlotte Street
London W1

N

National Association of Outdoor
Education
70 Victoria Road North
Heathwaite
Windermere, Westmorland

National Association of Youth Clubs
30 Devonshire Street
London W1

National Buildings Records
Fielden House
Great College Street
London SW1

National Caving Association
Department of Geography
University of Birmingham
Birmingham

National Coastal Rescue Training
Centre, Afan Lido
Aberavon, Glamorgan

National Rural and Environmental
Studies Association
c/o Chorley College of Education
Union Street
Chorley, Lancashire

National School Sailing Association
Education Office, County Hall
Chichester, Sussex

National Ski Federation
118 Eaton Square
London SW1

National Trust
42 Queen Anne's Gate
London SW1

National Trust for Scotland
5 Charlotte Square
Edinburgh 2

Nature Conservancy
19 Belgrave Square
London SW1

O

Outward Bound Trust
Iddesleigh House
Caxton Street
London SW1

R

Ramblers' Association
1/4 Crawford Mews
York Street
London W1H 1PT

Ramblers' Association Services
124 Finchley Road
London NW3

Royal Life Saving Society
14 Devonshire Street
London W1N 2AT

Royal National Lifeboat Institution
42 Grosvenor Gardens
London SW1

Royal Society for the Prevention of
Accidents
Royal Oak Centre
Brighton Road
Purley, Surrey CR2 2UR

Royal Society for the Protection of
Birds
The Lodge
Sandy, Bedfordshire

Royal Yachting Association
5 Buckingham Gate
London SW1E 6JT

S

St John Ambulance Association &
Brigade
1 Grosvenor Crescent
London SW1

School Journey Association of London
23 Southampton Place
London WC1A 2BT

School Natural Science Society
2 Bramley Mansions, Berrylands
Surbiton, Surrey

Scottish Field Studies Association
141 Bath Street
Glasgow C2

Scottish Tourist Board
2 Rutland Place, West End
Edinburgh

Scottish Youth Hostels Association
7 Globe Crescent
Stirling

Scout Association
25 Buckingham Palace Road
London SW1

Sports Council
26 Park Crescent
London W1N 4AJ

Sports Council for Scotland
4 Queensferry Street
Edinburgh EH2 4PB

Sports Council for Wales
National Sports Centre
Sophia Gardens
Cardiff CF1 9SE

Surf Life Saving Association
4 Cathedral Yard
Exeter

Swimming Teachers' Association
1 Birmingham Road
West Bromwich
Staffs

T
Thames Conservancy
Burdett House, 15 Buckingham Street
London WC2

W
Wales Tourist Board
3 Castle Street
Cardiff

Y
Young Men's Christian Association
51 Victoria Street
St Albans, Herts

Young Naturalists Association
Red House Field Centre, Hadness
Scarborough, Yorks

Young Women's Christian
Association
2 Weymouth Street
London W1N 4AX

Youth Hostels Association
(England and Wales)
Trevelyan House, 8 St Stephen's Hill
St Albans, Herts

Appendix B Facilities for residential courses

British Travel Association
64 St James Street
London SW1

Brochures available;
caravan and camping sites and
farmhouse accommodation, inexpensive
accommodation in Greater London.

Council for Environmental
Education
9 Devereux Court
London WC2R 3JR

*Directory of Centres for Outdoor
Studies in England and Wales.*

Countryside Holidays Association
Birch Heys, Cromwell Range
Manchester M14 6HO

Free brochure.

Field Studies Council
9 Devereux Court
London WC2R 3JR

Organized courses at various levels,
early March–late October.

Forestry Commission
25 Savile Row
London W1

Camp sites available in forest
parks.

Geographical Association
343 Fulwood Road
Sheffield 10

Directories of centres for field
study and of local authority
field centres.

Holiday Fellowship Ltd
Fellowship House
142 Great North Way
Hendon, London NW4

Free brochure.

Methodist Guild Holidays
2 Chester House, Pages Lane
Muswell Hill
London N10

Free brochure.

Northern Ireland Tourist Board
11 Berkeley Street
London W1

Free accommodation list.

Outward Bound Trust
Iddesleigh House, Caxton Street
London SW1

Applications for courses, normally
26 days duration, at one of six
schools.

Sports Council 26 Park Crescent London W1N 4AJ	Residential courses available at four sports centres and two specialist centres – both 'closed' and 'open' courses.
Sports Council for Scotland 4 Queensferry Street Edinburgh EH2 4PE	Applications for course details to the Council Administration.
Sports Council for Wales National Sports Centre Sophia Gardens Cardiff CF1 9SE	Applications for course details to the Council Administration.
Scottish Tourist Board 2 Rutland Place, West End Edinburgh	*Where to Stay in Scotland* (booklet).
Wales Tourist Board 3 Castle Street Cardiff	*Where to Stay in Wales* (booklet).
Young Men's Christian Association 51 Victoria Street St Albans, Herts	Free brochure.
Young Women's Christian Association 2 Weymouth Street London W1N 4AX	Free directory.
Youth Hostels Association (England and Wales) Trevelyan House 8 St Stephen's Hill St Albans, Herts	*Youth Hostels for Field Studies* (free leaflet).
Youth Service Information Centre Humberstone Drive Leicester LE5 ORG	*Conference Centres* and *Holidays for Youth* (booklets).

Appendix C First aid kits

First aid kit – day requirements

First aid manual
Assorted adhesive dressings
Assorted roller bandages
Assorted prepared sterile dressings
2 triangular bandages
1 crêpe bandage 3″ wide
1 pair scissors (blunt-nosed)
1 pair small forceps
1 packet safety pins (rustless, assorted)
Lint (pre-packed)
White gauze (pre-packed)
Paper tissues
Sanitary towels
Disposal bag

Acriflavine
Antiseptic (e.g. Dettol)
Anti-histamine ointment
Anti-midge preparation
Anti-sting relief ointment
Paracetamol
Smelling salts (e.g. sal volatile)

First aid kit – extended visit

First aid manual
1 pair scissors (blunt-nosed)
1 pair forceps
1 set lightweight splints
1 packet needles
1 packet safety pins (rustless, assorted)
1 hot-water bottle

6 triangular bandages
3 crêpe bandages 3″ wide
Roller bandages – various widths
Assorted adhesive dressings
Adhesive strapping roll 1″ wide
Prepared sterile dressings – various sizes

1 medicine glass (unbreakable)
2 medicine dispensing spoons
1 small pressure stove and kettle
2 small kidney bowls
3 small towels
Sanitary towels
Paper tissues
1 Thermos flask
Disposal bags

White and pink (boracic) lint ⎫ in
White gauze   ⎬ small
Cotton wool   ⎭ packets

90

Antiseptic (e.g. Dettol)
Calamine lotion
Liniment
Potassium permanganate
Smelling salts (e.g. sal volatile)
Surgical spirit
Witch-hazel

Acriflavine
Anti-histamine ointment
Anti-midge preparation
Anti-sting relief ointment
Bicarbonate of soda
Boric ointment
Burn jelly
Oil of cloves

Paracetamol
Indigestion tablets
Liquid paraffin
Vegetable laxative
Throat lozenges
Gargle solution

Appendix D Governing bodies of sport: certificates and coaching awards

Land-based activities

Caving	Cave Leadership Training Board 5 St Paul's Street Leeds	Cave Leaders' Certificate
Mountaineering	British Mountaineering Council 26 Park Crescent London W1N 4EE	Professional Guides' Certificate
	Mountain Leadership Training Board Sports Council 26 Park Crescent London W1N 4AJ	Mountain Leadership Certificate
	Scottish Mountain Leadership Training Board Sports Council for Scotland 4 Queensferry Street Edinburgh EH2 4PB	Mountain Leadership Certificate. Mountaineering Instructors' Certificate. A Winter Certificate is awarded in Scotland.
	Northern Ireland Mountain Leadership Training Board c/o Sports Council 49 Malone Road Belfast BT9 6RZ	Mountaineering Instructors' Advanced Certificate
Orienteering	British Orienteering Federation 3 Glenfinlas Street Edinburgh 3	Courses for advanced training for competitors, controllers, and setters.
Riding	British Horse Society The National Equestrian Centre Stoneleigh Kenilworth, Warwicks	*Professional instructors* British Horse Society Assistant Instructor, British Horse Society Instructor,

		Fellowship of the British Horse Society.
		Riding clubs Series of proficiency tests Grade I–IV.
		Pony clubs Series of proficiency tests.
Ski-ing	National Ski Federation 118 Eaton Square London SW1	*Coaching awards* Pre-Ski Organiser, Pre-Ski Instructor, Artificial Ski Slope Instructor, National Grade 3 – Assistant Ski Instructor, National Grade 2 – Ski Instructor, National Grade 1 – Ski Teacher.

Water-based activities

Angling	National Anglers Council Peakirk Peterborough, Northants	No coaching or performance awards, but the NAC is considering the establishment of syllabuses for coaching standards.
Canoeing	British Canoe Union, Room 315 26 Park Crescent London W1N 4DT	*Tests of proficiency* Elementary Canoeing Test (kayak or Canadian), Inland Proficiency Test (kayak or Canadian), Sea Proficiency Test (kayak), Advanced Inland Test (kayak or Canadian) Advanced Sea Test. *Coaching awards* Senior Instructor Award (inland, sea, or Canadian), Coach Award Senior Coach Award Specialist Coach Awards.
Rowing	Amateur Rowing Association 160 Great Portland Street London W1N 5TB	*Coaching awards* Basic Level, Club Level,

		Advanced Level (available from 1973).
Sailing	Royal Yachting Association Certificates Department 5 Buckingham Gate Westminster London SW1E 6JT	1. National Proficiency Certificate, 2. National Day-Boat (Elementary, Intermediate and Advanced) Certificates, 3. National Coastal Certificate, 4. National Motor Launch and Power Boat Certificate, 5. Advanced or Instructors' Certificate for Day Boats, 6. National Offshore Sailing Certificate.
	National School Sailing Association Education Office County Hall Chichester, Sussex	1. Instructors' Certificate. 2. Sailing Master/Senior Instructor Certificate. 3. Coach Certificate.
Surfing	Surf Life Saving Association of Great Britain 4 Cathedral Yard Exeter	1. *Sea survival* (open to everyone) a. Preliminary b. Surf competence c. Advanced 2. *Beach Competence* (open to everyone) a. Resuscitation b. Elementary c. Qualified Certificate d. Distinction 3. *Water Competence* (restricted to affiliated club members) Bronze, Silver, and Gold Medallions 4. *Instructor Awards* (restricted to affiliated club members)
Swimming	Amateur Swimming Association	Proficiency Awards in Swimming at Bronze,

94

	Acorn House 314 Grays Inn Road London WC1	Silver, and Gold standards; Proficiency Awards in Personal Survival at Bronze, Silver, and Gold standards.
	Royal Life Saving Society 14 Devonshire Street London W1N 2AT	1. Safety Awards – Water Safety Preliminary and Advanced. 2. Resuscitation Awards – Preliminary and Advanced. 3. Life-Saving Awards: Elementary Award Intermediate Award Bronze Medallion Sub-Aqua Bronze Medallion Bronze Cross Award of Merit Distinction Diploma. 4. Life Guard Corps Proficiency Award 5. Teachers' Certificate Advanced Teachers' Certificate
Under-water swimming	British Sub Aqua Club 160 Great Portland Street London W1N 5TB	*Coaching awards* Snorkel Instructors' Certificate (for teachers), BSAC Instructor: Club Instructor Advanced Instructor National Instructor. *Diving qualifications* Third Class, Second Class, First Class.
Water ski-ing	British Water Ski Federation 22 Station Approach Virginia Water, Surrey	BWSF arranges courses for instructors, satisfactory attendance at which indicates competence to instruct others at appropriate level.

Appendix E   Codes of conduct

THE COUNTRY CODE	Originally prepared by members of the National Parks Commission. A simple list of rules laid down to encourage visitors to the countryside to realize that their own responsibilities are the condition of their enjoyment of the countryside.	*Published by:* HMSO *Available from:* Government bookshops or through any bookseller
THE GREEN CROSS CODE	This code supersedes the kerb drill introduced when traffic densities and speeds were quite different from today. It is presented in a simple sequence of six points, each of which requires explanation if the maximum effect is to be gained. Once the meaning of the code is understood, the steps are straightforward. Excellent pictorial aids are available, including a Green Cross Code film.	*Published by:* Royal Society for the Prevention of Accidents *Available from:* Royal Society for the Prevention of Accidents Royal Oak Centre Brighton Road Purley, Surrey CR2 2UR
THE HIGHWAY CODE	This is a practical guide to the problems met in driving, walking, or cycling. The code explains the right way of behaving on roads for the road user on foot, on wheels, and also on the motorway; provides rules for cyclists, as well as sections on animals, and on railway level crossings. A detailed appendix provides valuable additional information.	*Published by:* HMSO *Available from:* Government bookshops or through any bookseller

THE MOUNTAIN CODE	Produced at the suggestion of the British Mountaineering Council to provide guidance for all people wishing to enjoy the hills and to have respect for the ideals of conservation and the rights of landowners.	*Published by:* Sports Council *Available from:* Sports Council Sports Council for Scotland Sports Council for Wales (see Appendix A for addresses)
THE OUTDOOR STUDIES CODE	Written to remind those who are planning and undertaking field studies of their special responsibilities, personal safety, respect for the interests of others, and conservation of the areas used. Useful facts concerning access to land and rights of way are presented along with information on facilities and records.	*Published by:* Council for Environmental Education *Available from:* Secretary of Resources Committee Council for Environmental Education 9 Devereux Court, Strand London WC2R 3JR
THE WATER SPORTS CODE	Sets out simply and clearly a general code for all water users and for individual activities involving recreational interests of inland waters, including: angling, canoeing, motor boating (including small craft and cruisers), rowing, sailing, underwater swimming and diving, water ski-ing.	*Published by:* Sports Council *Available from:* Sports Council Sports Council for Scotland Sports Council for Wales

Appendix F   A selection of useful publications

General

BARRELL, G. R. *Teachers and the Law*. Methuen, 1966.
CAMPBELL, I. *Law of Footpaths*. Commons, Open Spaces and Footpaths Preservation Society, 1968.
CREBER, F. L. *Safety for Industry*. Queen Anne Press for RoSPA, 1967.
Department of Education and Science.
  Health of the School Child 1969–70. (Report of the Chief Medical Officer). HMSO, 1972.
  Safety at School (Education Pamphlet No. 53). HMSO, 1967.
  Safety in Outdoor Pursuits (Safety Series No. 1). HMSO, 1972.
Dunlop PE Handbook. Education Section, Dunlop Ltd, 1971.
ELLIS, MAURICE. *Accidents to Children*. Evans Bros, 1967.
FLORIO, A. E. and STAFFORD, GEORGE T. *Safety Education*. McGraw-Hill, 3rd edn, 1969.
HUNT, J. H. *Accident Prevention and Life Saving*. Livingstone, 1965.
Safety Education. RoSPA. (Three times yearly)
Your Weather Service. HMSO, 3rd edn, 1959.
Youth Hostels for School Journey Parties. Youth Hostels Association. (Leaflet)

First Aid

ABC of First Aid. British Red Cross Society, rev. edn, 1968.
Digest of First Aid. St John Ambulance Association, 1970.
GARDNER, A. WARD and ROYLANCE, P. J. *New Essential First Aid*. Pan Books, 1967.
Junior First Aid Manual. British Red Cross Society, rev. edn, 1972.
MILES, STANLEY and ROYLANCE, P. J. *Teaching First Aid*. Bailliere, Tindall & Cassell, 1970.
[*Senior*] *First Aid Manual:* the authorised manual of St John Ambulance, St Andrew's Ambulance Association, British Red Cross Society. St John Ambulance Association/British Red Cross Society, 3rd edn, 1972.

Camping, Caving, and Mountain Safety

BLACKSHAW, A. *Mountaineering: from Hill Walking to Alpine Climbing*. Penguin Books, 1966.
CULLINGFORD, C. H. D. (ed.) *British Caving: an Introduction to Speleology*. Routledge & Kegan Paul, 2nd edn, 1962.

98

CULLINGFORD, C. H. D. *Manual of Caving Techniques*. Routledge & Kegan Paul, 1969.

Department of Education and Science.
Camping (Education Pamphlet No. 58). HMSO, 1971.
Safety in Outdoor Pursuits (Safety Series No. 1). HMSO, 1972, chapter 1.

DISLEY, JOHN (ed.) *Expedition Guide: the Duke of Edinburgh Award Scheme*. Duke of Edinburgh Award, 3rd rev. edn, 1971.

Exposure (Pamphlet 380). British Mountaineering Council, rev. edn, 1968.

Handbook for Expeditions: a Planning Guide. Brathay Exploration Group/ Geographical Magazine, 1971.

JACKSON, JOHN. *Safety on Mountains*. Central Council of Physical Recreation, rev. edn, 1968.

LANGMUIR, E. *Mountain Leadership*. Scottish Council of Physical Recreation, Edinburgh, 1969.

Map Reading Manual (Army Department).
Part I: Map Reading. HMSO, 1955.
Part II: Air Photo Reading. HMSO, 1958
Part III: Field Sketching. HMSO, 1957.

Mountain Rescue (Training Handbook RAF Mountain Rescue Teams). HMSO, 2nd edn, 1968.

Mountain Rescue and Cave Rescue. Mountain Rescue Committee. (Annually)

WILLIAMS, P. F. *Camping and Hill Trekking*. Pelham Books, 1969.

WRIGHT, J. E. B. and MURRAY, W. *The Technique of Mountaineering*. Kaye & Ward, 1964.

Overseas Travel

Education Exchange. Central Bureau for Educational Visits and Exchanges. (Three times yearly)

Hints on Conducting School Parties Abroad. School Travel Service, rev. edn, 1971.

How to Organise a First Holiday Abroad for a Youth Group. National Association of Youth Clubs, 1967. (Leaflet)

Information for Party Leaders. British India Steam Navigation Co. (Annually)

School and Youth Group Holidays. Youth Hostels Association. (Annually)

Vacation Courses Abroad. Central Bureau for Educational Visits and Exchanges. (Annually)

Working Holidays. Central Bureau for Educational Visits and Exchanges. (Annually)

Youth and Student Travel. Central Bureau for Educational Visits and Exchanges. (Annually)

Youth Visits Abroad. Central Bureau for Educational Visits and Exchanges. (Annually)

Road Safety

AA Members Handbook. Automobile Association. (Every two years)
COHEN, J. and PRESTON, B. *Causes and Prevention of Road Accidents*. Faber, 1968.
Driving: the Ministry of Transport Manual. HMSO, 1970.
Good Riding (*Motor Cycling*). Royal Society for the Prevention of Accidents, rev. edn, 1971.
Research on Road Safety. HMSO, 1965.
Riding Code. British Horse Society, 1971.
Road Accident Annual Reports. HMSO.
Road Accident Statistics. RoSPA. (Annually)
Road Craft: Police Drivers' Manual. HMSO, 2nd edn, 1968.
ROBERTS, PETER. *Better Cycling*. Kaye & Ward, 1969.
Royal Automobile Club Guide and Handbook. RAC. (Annually)
Skilful Cycling. RoSPA, rev. edn, 1964.
Turn to Better Driving. RoSPA, rev. edn, 1971.

Water Safety

Admiralty Tide Tables. Hydrographer to the Navy. (Distributed by J. D. Potter)
BULL, J. W. *An Introduction to Safety at Sea*. Brown, Son & Ferguson, 1966.
Department of Education and Science. *Safety in Outdoor Pursuits* (DES Safety Series No. 1). HMSO, 1972, chapter 2.
Life Saving and Water Safety. Royal Life Saving Society, 1969.
National School Sailing Association
    Safety Afloat.
    Cold Can Kill.
    Safety Boats, Parts 1 and 2.
National Water Safety Committee. *A Guide for Local Authorities on the Organisation of Accident Prevention in and on Water*. RoSPA, 1969.
On the Water, In the Water. RoSPA, rev. edn, 1971.
SANDERS, G. *Canoeing for Schools and Youth Groups*. British Canoe Union, 2nd edn, 1970.
The Sea in Education. HMSO, 1964.
Tide Currents and Beach Safety: Notes for Lifeguards. Advisory Committee on Beach Life Saving for Devon and Cornwall.
Tide Tables. British Transport Docks Board. (Annually)